The Capacity Contract

. . . .

Intellectual Disability and the Question of Citizenship

Stacy Clifford Simplican

University of Minnesota Press
Minneapolis
London

An abbreviated version of chapter 1 was published as "The Capacity Contract: Locke, Disability, and the Political Exclusion of 'Idiots,'" *Politics, Groups, and Identities* 2, no. 1 (2014): 90–103. An abbreviated version of chapter 4 was published as "A Narrative Inquiry of Self Advocacy: Rethinking Empowerment from Liberal Sovereignty to Arendtian Spontaneity," *Disability Studies Quarterly* 33, no. 3 (2013), www.dsq-sds.org /article/view/3244.

Published by the University of Minnesota Press
111 Third Avenue South, Suite 290
Minneapolis, MN 55401-2520
http://www.upress.umn.edu

Library of Congress Cataloging-in-Publication Data

Simplican, Stacy Clifford.
The capacity contract : intellectual disability and the question of citizenship /
Stacy Clifford Simplican.
Includes bibliographical references and index.
ISBN 978-0-8166-9397-9 (hc)—ISBN 978-0-8166-9403-7 (pb)
1. People with mental disabilities—Civil rights.   2. People with mental
disabilities—Political activity.   3. Cognition disorders—Political aspects.
4. Political rights.   5. Political participation.   6. Citizenship.   I. Title.
HV3004.S54   2015
323.3—dc23   2014025338

Printed in the United States of America on acid-free paper

The University of Minnesota is an equal-opportunity educator and employer.

21 20 19 18 17 16 15   10 9 8 7 6 5 4 3 2 1

THE CAPACITY CONTRACT

The fool hath said in his heart, there is no such thing as justice.

—THOMAS HOBBES, *LEVIATHAN*

Contents

Abbreviations

AAIDD	American Association on Intellectual and Developmental Disabilities
ADA	Americans with Disabilities Act
ASAN	Autistic Self Advocacy Network
ASD	autism spectrum disorder
CACL	Canadian Association for Community Living
CAMR	Canadian Association for the Mentally Retarded
CRPD	Convention on the Rights of Persons with Disabilities
IDD	intellectual and developmental disability
LEND	Leadership Education in Neurodevelopmental and Related Disabilities
Project ACTION	Accessible Community Transportation in Our Nation
SABE	Self Advocates Becoming Empowered
SDS	Society for Disability Studies
TAB	temporarily able-bodied
TAC	Treatment Action Campaign

Anxiety, Democracy, and Disability

IN NOVEMBER 2008, I attended my first self-advocacy meeting for people with intellectual and developmental disabilities. Held in the banquet room of a buffet restaurant, I expected to find self-advocates telling stories of institutional abuse and demanding political rights. Instead, I found nondisabled staff members and advisers orchestrating a meeting that mainly consisted of taking the roll and reading last month's minutes. When people with intellectual and developmental disabilities actually participated in the meeting, they often parroted lines told to them by staff. If they managed to raise an objection, nondisabled advisers and staff easily shut them down. In general, people with intellectual and developmental disabilities seemed more interested in eating dinner after the meeting than in any form of political consciousness-raising.

During dinner, I found myself engaged in conversation with a man sitting diagonally across from me. Charles,[1] an older black man, wore a dark-blue parka the entire evening. His speech was difficult to understand—both soft-spoken and slurred—and so I often asked him to repeat himself, trying to avoid nodding along to stories that I pretended to hear. But I sensed that my constant interruptions frustrated him, and eventually our conversation became less documented by words and more occupied with smiling at each other, smiling at our food, and then smiling back at each other.[2] He boasted about how much he had eaten (pointing to three plates of food, each plate now stacked on top of another) and how much Coke he had drunk (pointing at each empty glass: "One ... two ... three ... four"). With a broad smile and his hands patting his stomach, I assumed Charles was reflecting on a good meal, despite the overall blandness of the buffet. "One time," he began, and then related a story about how much he enjoyed sleeping and about a particular day when he was so tired he did not want to get out of bed. I waited for the story's climax, but after a while, I realized that his story was, somehow, complete.

The conversation puzzled me and, in many ways, epitomized my general discontent with the entire evening. Where was the political agency I expected to find? I had formed my high expectations based on national disability rights conferences, where leaders of the self-advocacy movement articulated a political mission centered on enhancing political agency. But the people with intellectual and developmental disabilities at this meeting seemed more interested in eating dinner than changing key elements in their lives. All of them resided in group homes—the same kind of setting the larger self-advocacy movement has attacked for isolating people with disabilities from the broader community. And why was this man boasting to me about drinking four glasses of Coke? My inability to see how this meeting fostered political agency left me disappointed for the legitimacy of self-advocacy.

Even more distressing to me, however, was my own anxiety. My evening at the buffet dinner marked the first time I had been in close contact with so many adults with intellectual and developmental disabilities. I had presumed that my integration into these settings would be relatively simple. Indeed, I had assumed that my experience as an older sibling to my brother with autism had somehow made me conversant with all kinds of people with intellectual and developmental disabilities. Entirely nonverbal, often aggressive, and detached from many behavioral norms, my brother had familiarized me with profound disability.[3] I assumed this familiarity could easily travel, as if it had made me a kind of cosmopolitan of cognitive difference.

I was wrong.

In addition to being anxious about my engagement with Charles, I was self-conscious of how my engagement looked to others around me. Beside me, and directly across from Charles, sat a young black woman. Her unidentified ability status troubled me. Was she a staff member or a self-advocate with an intellectual disability? If she was nondisabled, I worried that she would find my pretense of understanding Charles especially distasteful, worn as it was on my outsider white self, sent from the nearby private university to collect observations. The fact that her ambivalent status troubled me *troubled* me even more, as my anxiety swirled in a muddled entanglement of disability, race, class, gender, sex, and privilege. My need to discern disability—and its accompanying anxiety—seldom abated as I repeatedly found myself engaging with people whose disability status was ambiguous.

For disability studies scholars, my anxiety stems from a larger ableist culture that privileges a fictive ideal of health, stability, and strength amid the bodily realities of vulnerability, decay, and death.[4] As such, disability arouses fear, disgust, pity, and anxiety.[5] Although one in five people will experience disability in her life, the public presence of disabled people still manages to cause surprise.[6] What causes this anxiety? For Harlan Hahn, our anxiety about disability is both aesthetic and existential. Aesthetic anxiety refers to fears about physical bodily differences and the perceived failures of some bodies to attain norms of perfection.[7] Existential anxiety stems from the fear that disability will erode human capacities that are essential to human flourishing and human relationships.[8]

In *The Capacity Contract*, I argue that entrenched anxieties about disability are not only aesthetic and existential but also political, as disability reveals the deep discrepancy between the ways we conceptualize the demands of political participation and the actual range of ways people act politically. My anxiety emerges from the discordance between the ways we as democratic citizens idealize cognitive capacity as a trusted democratic resource and our realization of the profound vulnerabilities besetting our cognitive capabilities. Democracy entails that we imagine that the most important political duties are cognitive tasks, such as reasoning, reflection, judgment, and deliberation. For political decisions to be legitimate, we expect people to reason sufficiently about themselves, the world around them, and the political futures they desire. People with intellectual and developmental disabilities subvert these idealized cognitive expectations as well as the fictive political subject from which they emerge. As such, people with intellectual and developmental disabilities fuel democratic anxieties because they symbolize the defects of democratic reasoning. Deprived of political standing, their claims of injustice are like the tales of Shakespeare's idiot, "full of sound and fury, signifying nothing."[9]

In retelling the story of my own anxiety, my aim is not to pathologize democratic anxiety and eradicate it; instead, we can use anxiety as a prompt, causing us to rethink our relationship to disability and democracy. Thus, by making this anxiety ours, and by using words like "we" and "us," I mean to capture all of us: disabled, nondisabled, and all of the ambiguity in between.[10] Importantly, just as disability studies scholars reframe disability from biologically determined to culturally produced, our anxiety about disability is manufactured—created from histories of segregation, ableist norms, and entrenched prejudice. For Rosemarie Garland-Thomson, "Unpredictable or indecipherable cues *create* anxiety. It is not that disability itself creates unease, but rather people's inability to read such cues disrupts the expected, routine nature of social relations."[11] Unraveling this anxiety is difficult. First, when disabled people express positive perspectives on their own lives, nondisabled people simply disbelieve them.[12] Second, research finds that abled *and* disabled people report similar levels of implicit bias toward disability.[13] Hence, nondisabled people do not *own* ableism any more than disabled people do; we share it, whoever *we* are.

In fact, no human can emulate the disciplined and idealized cognitive demands of the fictive democratic subject, and yet we maintain it as a model of democratic politics. This ideal subject exists alongside democracy's commitment to protect the equality of all persons, regardless of capacity. Indeed, the story of disability and democracy is not a monolithic tale of oppression,[14] as vulnerability also invites solidarity, strength, and new ways to imagine citizenship.[15]

Our allegiance to equality *and* an ideal cognitive subject reveals a deep tension in democratic theory that I conceptualize as two sides of a *capacity contract* that pulls democracy to both embrace and expel vulnerability. The first side of the capacity contract bases political membership on a threshold level of capacity and excludes anyone who falls below. In doing so, the capacity contract naturalizes a fictional account of *compulsory capacity* that none of us can achieve. Our inability to conform to the fictional subject leaves us with a deep anxiety, arising between the demands of democratic participation and our inability to meet them. The other side of the capacity contract, however, sees incapacity as essential to human life and thus bases democratic solidarity on shared human vulnerability. Although the thrust of *The Capacity Contract* embraces the latter and more democratic capacity contract, it also acknowledges that democratic citizens cannot easily discard the first and more exclusionary contract. Because we politically mobilize amid both capacity contracts, we should expect anxiety around exclusion and solidarity to surface often—in the history and contemporary writings of political thought, as well as in the political movements and rhetoric around us.

My concept of the capacity contract builds on the burgeoning field of critical social contract theory, which interrogates dominant norms of equality for underlying systems of oppression. Pioneered by Carole Pateman's sexual contract, which hinges fraternal equality on women's subordination, and Charles Mills's racial contract, critical social contract theory reveals how domination operates across liberal democratic theories.[16] Like the racial contract, the goal of the capacity contract is domination and disappearance. Disappearance accomplishes two objectives. First, it enables the social contract to appear universal—as if we were created cognitively equal—despite hinging on a distinction between the cognitively abled and the cognitively disabled. Second, in contemporary politics, this disappearance serves to contain anxiety about our obligations to people with severe disabilities and the threat they pose to societal resources. And though the capacity contract may aim for erasure, it nevertheless fails, as we remain anxious about our own and each other's cognitive abilities in the face of an ever-complex governance order.

In this book, I counter democratic anxiety and exclusion in two ways. First, I examine key theorists of the social contract and liberal democracy to show how both sides of the capacity contract operate in their work. As theorists of equality, they require a unit of analysis, and this forces them to measure people according to cognitive capacity. Even when democratic theorists aim to be inclusive, they too often hinge democratic solutions to the cognitive capacities of citizens, thus reinforcing the exclusion of and stigma against people with intellectual disabilities. By showing how our theories manufacture both the construction of disability and our anxiety of it, we can begin to detach democratic membership from individual measures of cognitive capacity.

My second aim is to re-signify self-advocates' actions—which at first may seem apolitical and uncoordinated—as legitimate modes of democratic action. I base my conclusions on my observations from local, state, and national disability rights events. Although self-advocates often stake inclusion on claiming cognitive competence, this move unintentionally recasts exclusion and stigma on others who are more severely impaired. In contrast, when people with intellectual disabilities and their allies gather in public settings—from hotel lobbies to buffet restaurants—they contest the prejudicial belief that disabled lives are miserable and best kept hidden.

Although I failed to recognize it at the time, Charles was telling me a story about freedom. It took me over a year to understand the political significance behind his boasts about how many cups of Coke he drank, and another three years before I understood the import of his story about sleep. As my understanding of our conversation evolved, I also began to reevaluate that entire November evening. I began to see an alternative account of political participation in the combined public presence of nondisabled staff members and people with intellectual and developmental disabilities. Even people with profound intellectual disabilities—that small class of people who even the most ardent theorists of disability rights claim can only be served by surrogates[17]—offer us ways to rethink democracy.

My beliefs in this democratic potential evolved as I became more involved with the self-advocacy movement: I volunteered at an advocacy office for the next year and a half, and I continued to attend local, state, and national disability rights meetings and events. Through this, I began an earnest conversation with parents, siblings, and leaders in the self-advocacy movement about how to advance the rights of people with the most severe intellectual disabilities. To understand this democratic potential, however, we need to confront how our anxiety about intellectual disability infiltrates emancipatory politics.

Defining Approaches to Intellectual Disability

Re-envisioning democratic politics and people with profound forms of intellectual disabilities is not easy; much lies in the way. When faced with questions of politics and intellectual disability, we primarily ask one of two questions: First, does this person measure up to the duties of citizenship? And if not, who is responsible for this person's care? The first question aims to measure the severity of the intellectual disability in order to situate the person along a continuum of citizenship. The other question focuses on the kind of care the person with the intellectual disability needs, who does the caring, and at what cost. For readers familiar with these theoretical debates, the works of John Rawls and Eva Feder Kittay aptly capture these differences.[18] Importantly, measurement and care accounts often merge into each other. Care theorists often specify the possession of certain capacities—attentiveness, listening, patience—whereas measurement folks depend on care to instill a threshold level of capacity in future generations, or rely on care for those who cannot.

These questions, though important, forestall other ways of thinking about Charles and fail to grapple with the anxiety he poses to democratic norms. Indeed, critical disability studies scholars reject both accounts, arguing that measurement belies the social construction and instability of disability[19] and that care disempowers disabled people through paternalism.[20] Proponents of measurement and care reflect insufficiently on the ways in which these approaches themselves define people with disabilities. My point is not that our answers to these questions have been erroneous but that the kinds of questions we ask diminish disability's significance for democracy.[21] Although disability studies scholars critique measurement and care, both approaches continue to affect the meaning and significance of disability.

Measuring Capacities / Containing Anxiety

In crucial respects, measurement inheres to the concept of intellectual disability, and so we should expect measurement to surface in almost every instantiation of the subject. Intellectual disability is comprehensible only when it connects to a nondisabled cognitive norm. Defining disability thus always incites a parallel question: disabled in comparison to what or to whom?[22] For instance, if transported into my shoes on that November evening, measurement folks might ask the following questions about Charles: *Is he rational enough to vote? Is he capable of understanding and acting in his own self-interest?* The answers to these questions would determine Charles's political standing. If sufficiently rational, Charles would join the ranks of full citizenship. He could vote; he could serve on a jury; he could run for office.[23] If more severely disabled, the measurement folks might recommend a surrogate—perhaps a caregiver or one of the many staff members that surrounded him that night—to represent him. Other proponents of measurement might gauge Charles's intellectual impairment so severe as to preclude political (and even human) status altogether.[24]

Even though measurement is inseparable from intellectual disability, activists and scholars actively resist it.[25] Critics associate measurement rubrics with the medical model of disability, which sharply distinguishes between disabled and nondisabled populations, views disability as

arising entirely out of bodily difference and deformity, and offers rehabilitation or eradication as the only solution. Measurement is central to
the medical model of disability, as followers presume they can objec-
tively rank human capabilities. The stigmatizing force of the medical
model led disability rights activists and scholars to develop the social
model of disability. Rather than view disability as a natural condition, the
social model approach indicts prejudicial attitudes, capitalism, and architectural barriers for constructing a subjected class of disabled persons.[26]
Although disability rights activists and scholars have championed the
social model of disability for decades, the medical model continues to
dominate disability discourses in the United States.[27] Indeed, Kristin
Bumiller argues that the biomedicalization of autism is evidence of a
resurgence of medical control over bodies, a move that is supported by
medical specialists and parents of autistic children.[28]

    Even amid attempts to resist it, however, the medical model helps us
define the category of people we want to consider. According to the
American Association on Intellectual and Developmental Disabilities
(AAIDD), intellectual disability is "characterized by significant limitations both in intellectual functioning (reasoning, learning, problem
solving) and in adaptive behavior, which covers a range of everyday social and practical skills."[29] Under this model, an IQ score between 70 and
75 indicates intellectual limitation. Developmental disabilities include
intellectual disability, but also encompass such conditions as autism
spectrum disorder (ASD), behavior disorders, brain injury, cerebral
palsy, Down syndrome, fetal alcohol syndrome, and spina bifida. When
I refer to intellectual disability in this book, I aim to capture people who
have intellectual disabilities and people with developmental disabilities
whose disability has an intellectual component.

    For as much as we rely on the medical model to define intellectual
disability—as a separate and definable category of existence—identifying
people with intellectual disabilities is far from straightforward, as my
dinner experience encapsulates. As my fieldwork progressed, I entered
new sites and encountered different sets of people, with and without
disabilities. As I describe in chapters 4 and 5, rarely does intellectual
disability come with a physical marker. Instead, I discerned intellectual
disability by communicating with other people, as confusing speech
patterns, muffled language, or broken norms of bodily distance or
touch signaled disability. But even here I learned to be cautious: indeci-

pherable speech is, at times, a sign of physical disability. Breaking norms of engagement can arise from different cultural customs, disability, or inconsiderateness. I learned to identify intellectual disability by watching others. Nondisabled people were far more likely to interrupt someone's speech if they perceived that person to be intellectually disabled.

Similarly, practitioners behind AAIDD recognize that our methods of measurement, as well as what we measure, change over time. For instance, categorizing subjects as learning disabled may make little sense in communities with high illiteracy and few educational supports.[30] In sharp contrast, Henry Goddard, a prominent figure during the eugenic era, ushered in an expansive class of mental deficiency, including "idiots," "imbeciles," and "morons." According to Goddard, mental deficiency was rampant among blacks, immigrants, and poor whites.[31]

Measuring and classifying people with intellectual disabilities, however contested, is extremely consequential. During the eugenic era, a diagnosis of cognitive impairment legitimized state-sponsored sterilization campaigns and permanent institutionalization of children and adults in overcrowded and understaffed asylums. Until 1975 in the United States, public schools could legally expel and refuse admission to children with disabilities. Subsequent to the landmark passage of the Americans with Disabilities Act in 1990, the Supreme Court's focus on whether litigants are indeed disabled has sparked controversy, as the court's narrow definition of disability has limited the legislation's reach.[32] And people with intellectual disabilities find themselves among children and felons as a persistent disenfranchised class.[33]

Measurement's legacy is mixed. On the one hand, we can use measurement to protect the rights of people with disabilities. Take, for example, the case of legal defense. Lawyers must represent the legal needs of their clients; thus, they need to know whether a client is capable of acting in her best interest.[34] A legal classification of intellectual disability exempts a person from the death penalty, as the Supreme Court has ruled it to be cruel and unusual punishment. Moreover, systems of classification helped foster the disability rights movement, as the segregation of disabled people by impairment type cultivated disabled group identities, leading to the first efforts of political mobilization.[35]

On the other hand, measurement's lethal legacy persists. Currently, over 90 percent of pregnancies with a prenatal diagnosis of Down syndrome end in abortion in the United States.[36] Assuming that the abortion rate of fetuses with Down syndrome has remained stable for the last twenty years, we can estimate that in the United States alone, there are over a million people with Down syndrome missing.[37] For people with intellectual disabilities who survive pregnancy, their bodies remain subject to radical medical interventions. In the case of Ashley X, her parents and doctors considered drastic medical intervention necessary, removing her breast buds and uterus. They argued that the procedure allowed Ashley to escape the painful process of puberty and, more importantly, remain small enough that her parents could continue caring for her at home. Undoubtedly, measurement matters.

Exactly because measurement inheres to the concept of intellectual disability—defining disability's scope, history, and the practices surrounding it—we should expect to find it in theoretical discussions that take up the issue of intellectual disability and democracy. In fact, we find measurement in a range of contemporary theories that, though not concerned with disability, draw on a threshold account of capacities to define citizenship. Put another way, even political theories that are not within a social contract tradition enforce their own versions of capacity contracts. We might divide these accounts into three categories: (1) those that define the threshold by explicitly excluding people with intellectual disabilities, (2) those that define the threshold and presume its universality by ignoring intellectual disabilities, and (3) those that strive to define the threshold as expansively as possible to include people with intellectual disabilities.

While chapter 3 takes up these categories in more detail, let me state here that, for political theorists, a large part of the problem with measurement is that it over-defines both the person with an intellectual disability and our purview of relevant theoretical questions. On the first matter, when we approach people with intellectual disabilities with an outstretched measuring stick, we repeat the worst flaws with the medical model: stripping the person down to their diagnosed flaw, refusing to see them as a complex person whose characteristics defy measurement, and judging them by their measured outcome. As with my evening at the buffet restaurant, and at advocacy settings afterward, I found it difficult to let go of my own measuring stick. My personal dilemma maps on to theoretical critiques of the social model of disability: even when they aim to be inclusive, disability scholars and disability rights activists often call upon cognitive norms of autonomy and empowerment that redraw the boundaries of personhood and reify exclusion.[38] On the second matter, when measurement exhausts the set of relevant political questions, we fail to question fully the significance of intellectual disability and its relationships to our theories. Asking if a surrogate should represent a person with an intellectual disability in the voting booth or on a jury is important. But we should not presume this exhausts the means of political participation possible for people with intellectual disabilities.

Measurement draws us in because it is an effective means to ease our own anxiety. As Licia Carlson points out, our philosophical role is one of the expert, gatekeeper, or classifier—all of which secures us in a cloak of measurement, indifference, and distance.[39] When we select measurement as a tool, we fail to reflect on its validity, presuming that it tells us something definitive and clear. Conversely, we might ask, why is this set of capabilities or rationality necessary? What if we turned the measurement tool on itself and asked, *why does it hold so much power over us?* This is precisely what critical disability studies scholars are striving to do: to challenge the way we measure and see disability as a way to upend the set of binaries on which it rests.[40] But measurement is seldom a tool to instill reflective qualities. Instead, its power is in bolstering and securing the norm, whatever that norm may be. And this explains why thinking critically about intellectual disability is so difficult. How can we think outside of measurement when measurement inheres to the concept?

Caring about Disability / Censuring Anxiety

If measurement captures the story of what intellectual disability has meant, then care has told us what to do about it. Care counters the impersonal touch of the measuring stick by replacing threshold accounts of citizenship with a foundation of universal human interdependence and vulnerability. If in my shoes at that dinner, care theorists' questions would be quite different from their measurement counterparts: *What are Charles's needs? Are staff members sufficiently attentive to his needs? Are his attendants appropriately cared for?* Rather than focus on individual capacities, care hinges on the relational dynamics between people.

Care is a dominant theme in the history of people with intellectual disabilities in the United States. Although we likely associate institutionalization with a lack of care, early advocates for people with mental illness and intellectual disabilities fought for the creation of government-sponsored residential schools and homes. Advocates like Dorothea Dix in the mid-nineteenth century described the deplorable living conditions for people with intellectual disabilities: chained in barns, locked in rooms, soiled with defecation, naked or with few clothes, and, at times, for sale to the lowest bidder.[41] State-funded residential homes and schools answered Dix's call to provide adequate care for people whose own families could not or would not care for them appropriately. Dix's crusade of care thus merged with the eagerness of medical doctors to create a new specialty for themselves. These medical doctors, educators, and psychologists argued that the creation of large-scale schools could rehabilitate high-grade "idiots" and return them to their communities. In this respect, efforts of care and measurement coalesced.

Failures in care, however, punctuate the history of people with intellectual disabilities. After World War II, conscientious objectors sent to work at state mental institutions exposed the overcrowded, unsanitary, understaffed, and abusive conditions facing people with intellectual disabilities.[42] In 1965, Senator Robert F. Kennedy described the Willowbrook State School for children with intellectual disabilities as a "snakepit." In 1966, Burton Blatt and Fred Kaplan published *Christmas in Purgatory*, photographing the abysmal conditions of five unnamed institutions for the intellectually disabled, describing them as "a hell on earth." Six years later, Geraldo Rivera televised the same appalling conditions. Recent media attention documents similar abusive conditions. Published between 2010 and 2011, the *New York Times* series "Abused and Used" has exposed a high number of unexplained deaths, reports of repeated sexual and physical abuse, and the overuse of psychotropic medicine in place of more effective therapies within the New York State Office for People with Developmental Disabilities. As suggested in one journalist's video title, *A Failure to Protect,* both the need for care and persistent failures in care frame our attention to people with intellectual disabilities.

We see care also in the scholarship of Eva Feder Kittay, whose work around dependency and an ethics of care largely influences contemporary philosophical queries surrounding intellectual disability. Kittay, like the broader tradition of care theory from which her work emerges, counters measurement approaches by emphasizing human interdependence rather than autonomy, thus understanding "the entire self as constituted, known, and maintained through relationship."[43] This focus on a relational ontology promotes in care theorists a focus "on the concrete and particular."[44] Accordingly, Kittay's lived experience of mothering Sesha, her profoundly disabled daughter, informs her theory, providing her with a "certain vantage point," which acts "as a tether that prevents [her] from wandering away from the lived reality."[45]

Despite Kittay's emphasis on lived reality, her work idealizes care in problematic ways.[46] Her model of an ideal caregiver revolves around her idea of the transparent self, who "does not allow its own needs or vision of the good to cloud its perception of another's needs, and so offers no resistance to its response to another."[47] These are steep demands, and Kittay recognizes them as such. "Of course, no self is ever truly transparent in this sense, but such transparency is a benchmark for the self-conception of the individual who cares for a dependent person."[48] As Shiloh Whitney describes, Kittay yokes caregivers to an impossible ideal.[49] Disability rights activists similarly criticize care theory, arguing that care ethicists' valorization of care overlooks the fact that caregivers often abuse people with disabilities.[50] This idealization thus falters on two counts: it risks stigmatizing caregivers who (inevitably) fail to be transparent, and it obscures abusive caregivers.

Kittay also idealizes disabled dependents. We see this in her description of her daughter: "Sesha's coin and currency is love. That is what she wishes to receive and that is what she reciprocates in spades."[51] On the one hand, Kittay's idealization of Sesha is understandable: Kittay works within a discipline that persistently dehumanizes people with disabilities. Positive accounts are rare and therefore imperative. Kittay is self-conscious of her own need to present Sesha positively, describing her own unwillingness to encounter Sesha through the eyes of those who see her with repugnance.[52] On the other hand, Kittay's argument that the ability of love allows her daughter's caregivers to reciprocate hinges care to emotional reciprocity. Requirements for reciprocity are especially dangerous for people with developmental disabilities—like autism—whose disability may foreclose typical norms of emotional closeness.[53]

More generally, when we look closely at work from philosophers who are interested in intellectual disabilities, we see a similar trend: many political theorists and philosophers who earnestly explore the issue of intellectual disability have done so because of familial connections to disability. Martha Nussbaum's *Frontiers of Justice* discusses her autistic nephew;[54] Michael Bérubé's work on disability arises out of his experience fathering a son with Down syndrome;[55] Roger Gottlieb's "The Tasks of Embodied Love" discusses the effect of raising a daughter with an intellectual disability;[56] and Sophia Isako Wong's thoughts about care form through her relationship with her brother, who has Down syndrome.[57] All of these theorists—some more than others—move between personal experience and normative theory to guide their critique. They avoid, however, naming this way of theorizing as a method.

Autoethnography is a kind of sociological method—arising out of grounded theory—that describes how theorists like Kittay have been writing about intellectual disability. Carolyn Ellis and Arthur Bochner describe autoethnography as an autobiographical genre of writing in which researchers use their personal experience as a way to understand larger cultural phenomena.[58] By exploring personal experience, autoethnography challenges positivist research and its construction of the objective researcher. Because the vulnerability of the researcher is a crucial component in autoethnography, it counters abstract philosophical discussions of intellectual disability, as the latter implicitly disconnect philosophers from their own corporeality.[59] In this way, autoethnography seems well suited for projects on disability, as both genres reject the disembodied and idealized subject.[60]

Indeed, autoethnography captures work within disability studies. Many disability scholars situate their work through their own experience of being or becoming disabled.[61] Thomas Couser argues for the importance of autobiography in the disability rights movement and in disability studies scholarship, arguing that it offers a "medium for counterdiscourse that challenges stereotypes and misconceptions."[62] Disabled performers similarly weave autobiography into performance to redefine disability.[63]

Thinking about theoretical texts methodologically helps us think more critically about the function of personal experience in relation to disability within and beyond disability studies. Indeed, we can see measurement and care coalesce in our desire to define our own and others' relationship to disability: if we care about disability, we must be in close proximity to it.[64] We measure our own relationship to disability—our own or that of our loved one—to explain why we care about it and why we can speak about it. The pull of defining our relationship to disability is so strong that to keep one's position occluded transgresses the expectations of our audience.[65] Although I too share in this self-disclosure, I am also skeptical of the ways in which self-disclosure operates.

For care theorists—or those that come to disability through their love of a family member—the methodological questions raised here include the following: How does the disclosure of personal experience influence our understanding of intellectual disability? What happens when theorists of intellectual disability are also family members of loved ones with a disability? What kinds of biases are more apt to arise when the persona of intellectual disability is always a theorist's child? As evident by my line of questioning, I suspect that these works—while intensely valuable to the development of my own scholarship—may in fact have the adverse effect of depoliticizing disability by continually cloaking it within a familial framework.

Scholars within disability studies also worry about the role of autoethnography and how the medical and social models of disability infiltrate discourse—even when we explicitly try to disrupt their discursive power. Because many disability scholars and activists embrace the social model of disability—which centers on the cultural production of disability and de-emphasizes the body—some scholars argue that the dominance of the social model works to silence individuals' experience of pain, shame, or frustration with their impairment.[66] Hence, although life writing is meant to disrupt dominant discourses, it often falls into familiar (and not so destabilizing) narratives of overcoming disability. Couser argues that autoethnography "speaks of a disability as a condition that is affirmative rather than catastrophic," thus encoding proper discursive tones for disabled subjects.[67] As disability studies scholar David Mitchell warns, "there are dangers in the autobiographical turn," including authors' tendencies to emphasize dominant discourses of "rugged individualism" and ignore the structural elements that shape their identities.[68] Hence, autobiographical approaches seem to prescribe how a person relates to his disabled identity.

Jan Walmsley similarly worries about researchers who study people with intellectual disabilities. In particular, because most researchers who study self-advocacy share the same goals as the self-advocacy movement,

Walmsley argues that scholars produce a "somewhat uniform representation of people with admirable human qualities struggling to make the most of difficult lives." As Walmsley notes, this "may be replacing one stereotype with another."[69] Can we care about disability without romanticizing people with intellectual disabilities?

But I worry also about how the self-disclosure of disabled identity within disability studies may undermine the field's desire to destabilize the abled/disabled binary.[70] Defining oneself puts reader and author in relationship to one another, as if we can only understand the text if we know the status of the author. We are compelled to measure our self and the reader by abled/disabled categories, thus always loading the language—of "we" and "us"—in unspoken but easily recognized labels of disabled or abled. Consequently, autobiography helps contain our anxiety for disability. When authors disclose their disability, it is often as someone who identifies as disabled or who loves someone who is disabled. Care sidesteps anxiety by nestling our analysis in familial relations, often constructing dependency workers as transparently benevolent and developmentally disabled dependents as lovingly joyful. Though I have focused on Kittay, the broader language of care theory may lack the internal tools necessary to wrestle adequately with anxiety and its relationship to democratic theory. For example, Daniel Engster describes caring as "everything we do directly to help others to meet their basic needs, develop or sustain their basic capabilities, and alleviate or avoid pain or suffering, in an attentive, responsive and respectful manner."[71] No doubt, the world would be a much better place if we had more of this kind of care, but by privileging pain avoidance, care outlooks may inadvertently stall other important ways of critique, such as destabilizing norms.[72] Moreover, from a care perspective, our anxiety over disability risks quick dismissal, construed as a morally bad response that we should eradicate. At times, anxiety may be a democratic resource. If so, then we need a research methodology that makes us anxious.

Challenging Identity

If we err by sidestepping our anxieties about disability, how do we profitably use this anxiety without essentializing it as residing within disability? Confronting ableist anxieties is, in fact, a central component of the broader self-advocacy movement—and it may be the toughest challenge the self-advocacy movement faces. Ari Ne'eman, a self-advocate in the Unites States, argues that societal prejudice undermines legal mandates for inclusion; stereotypes continue to characterize people with disabilities as pitiful and apoitical.[73] Indicting nondisabled prejudice for stalling the empowerment of people with disabilities is a common tactic within advocacy circles, but self-advocates may also play a part in maintaining norms of compulsory capacity. In order to launch the argument that they deserve political standing, self-advocates are forced to make claims about their own cognitive competence, hence undermining their political message that all people with intellectual disabilities are political actors worth listening to. To act without the legitimacy of cognitive competence is to occupy an "uninhabitable identification."[74]

In many ways, Ne'eman performs this political paradox as a rising leader in the movement, a point that I will return to in chapter 4. Ne'eman, an articulate young man who identifies on the autism spectrum disorder, has achieved national prominence, appointed by President Barack Obama to the National Council on Disability. His rise to prominence is due, in part, to his ability to articulate the demands of the movement. Even as Ne'eman describes the obstacles he has faced because of his disability, he may—in certain situations—pass as nondisabled. In these situations, Ne'eman's public presence conforms to dominant norms of democratic comportment. Better said, his disability may not trigger anxiety. While Ne'eman challenges the idea that people with intellectual disabilities are incapable of participating in politics, his success may bolster beliefs that intelligible political participation requires a threshold level of cognitive competence.

Ne'eman's assertion that people with intellectual disabilities are capable of the full demands of citizenship maps onto the broader history of the disability rights movement, which has largely staked political inclusion on the recognition of equality and the articulation of disability as a distinct political identity. The disability rights movement gained momentum in the 1970s, following the civil rights and women's rights movements, and disability rights activists similarly embraced consciousness-raising as a fundamental process of political identity.[75] According to O'Toole, "positioning oneself in relation to the lived disability experience" was a fundamental aspect of the disability rights movement, which "mandated publicly naming one's relationship to disability."[76] Indeed, creating a class of "people with disabilities" served to unite people with disparate impairments into a formidable political collective.[77]

Identity politics has similarly shaped disability studies. According to Sandahl and Auslinger, "disability studies is implicitly conceptualized as the study of a group of people . . . defined by shared experiences of discrimination and by its vital subculture."[78] Likewise, feminist disability theorist Rosemarie Garland-Thomson aims to "recast [disability] from a form of pathology to a form of ethnicity."[79] Identity thus becomes the fulcrum of politics, as disabled citizens are expected to mobilize around shared group interests. For disability studies scholar Tobin Siebers, "identity politics remains in my view the most practical course of action by which to address social injustices against minority peoples."[80]

Identity politics and the social model of disability infuse the disability rights movement with two requirements: first, individuals must conceptualize themselves as disabled and as members of an oppressed class; and second, they must demand political inclusion on the basis of their identity.[81] These requirements problematically assume that citizens must perform a heavy amount of self-awareness in order to participate in politics—attributes that some people with more profound forms of intellectual disability may be unable to articulate or understand. Moreover, Christine Kelly argues that a conception of disabled identity that centers on independence and rationality is due, in part, to the continued overprevalence of "white, educated, physically disabled men" in the disability movement in the global North, which works to marginalize the diversity of experiences of the disability community.[82] Finally, identity politics bolsters abled/disabled binaries, even as the field of disability studies aims to dislodge these dichotomies. Indeed, disability studies scholar Lennard J. Davis suggests that the concept of identity "has been played out."[83]

Although I did not realize it when I first encountered Charles, he is an effective self-advocate precisely because he disrupts dominant norms of political identity and comportment. Charles disrupted my expectations of proper dinner conversation: he was hard to hear, and I had difficulty discerning his words. We made our conversation work through impromptu signs and an on-the-spot private language of smiles, eyebrow raising, and belly patting. Our conversation had to forge new pathways of communication in order to be effective. Rather than see my gestures with Charles as a subpar conversation, disability studies scholar Brenda Jo Brueggemann invites us to consider how disabled people can help reinvent rhetorical standards in the public sphere.[84]

Seeing my story with Charles as a conversation fits nicely with a current conceptualization of democracy as deliberative theory. Deliberative democratic theory understands governance as a process in which citizens reach decisions through rational dialogue. We can think of deliberative democratic theory as a spectrum theory, ranging from ideal to critical. In ideal democratic theory, we imagine citizens as perfectly rational, able to process their own desires into rational and public arguments. By "public," theorists mean the ability to offer arguments that any person could understand. Critical deliberative theory is quite different, wherein theorists' starting point is exclusion and injustice.[85] Despite their differences, both ideal and critical theorists give us a picture of democracy as a conversation.

Thinking about democracy as a conversation, my evening with Charles takes on new significance. While some critical theorists have acknowledged that rational argument fails to circumscribe the range of political claims,[86] we have yet to mine fully the levels of difficulty and possibility that attend speech situations with people with intellectual disabilities.[87] As I continued to attend conferences and disability rights events, I found myself in similar circumstances: engaged with a conversation partner with whom I could not take anything for granted. I never knew the starting place for dialogue, and once begun, I learned that the conversation could easily break unspoken rules of conduct. The anxiety I felt, stemming from everyday norms of personal interaction, more broadly maps onto underlying norms of democratic comportment. For some theorists, the failure to share norms of communication threatens deliberative outcomes so steeply that we should simply exclude people with mental illness and disability.[88] Alternatively, we could challenge this attitude. We could turn our anxiety onto underlying norms, asking what we lose when we insist on enforcing order over inclusion.[89]

Rather than try to assuage the audience's anxiety, contemporary disability performers use anxiety in their performances to challenge dominant norms, such as the idea that selfhood equates to speaking ability and that the self must be in control of herself and her audience.[90] For instance, Brueggemann describes how a disabled performer whose speech is unintelligible intentionally makes the audience uncomfortable and thus insists that the audience take an active role, willing "to adapt in order to meet the ability of the speaker."[91] Disability invites not only a reinvention of the self, but a new relationship between audience and speaker.

In essence, we need a political movement that challenges the stability of identity and relational norms, as well as a research method that challenges the attitudes of the researcher and reader. As research shows, our negative attitudes about disability are strong and enduring. We need a way to hold our anxiety long enough to begin to understand it.[92] Political theory has tools to offer this endeavor. Rather than offer an empirical answer to solve the problem of anxiety, political theorists imagine alternative social realities as a way to disrupt damaging norms.[93] For Ian Hacking, part of this ability entails developing a new language about disability, a language that arises from the generative potential of storytelling rather than from theoretical arguments.[94] In essence, we need a methodological approach to disability that does something different from the approaches of measurement and care.

In this way, the sociological method of autoethnography offers creative avenues that I make in my own research. Personal experience, though valuable, should not be the only lens to scrutinize disability. Consequently, this book analyzes advocacy organizations and offers these analyses in narrative form. Reflecting on the voices and actions of people with intellectual disabilities to guide theory is imperative for multiple reasons. First, inclusion of disabled voices is congruent with the disability rights movement's motto of "nothing about us, without us," and rectifies scholarship about disability that excludes the involvement of disabled persons. Second, the inclusion of people with disabilities destabilizes a method of ideal theorizing that has promoted an exclusionary conception of being human.[95] Third, moving between personal experience and participant observations of advocacy networks is consistent with a long line of feminist theorizing that uses empirical inquiry to inform normative reflection.[96] Finally, relying on advocates' actions momentarily suspends the epistemological authority of the researcher with the intent of allowing the experiences of those most marginalized to guide the development of theoretical claims.[97]

As part of my research, I attended local, state, and national conferences convened around disability rights between the fall of 2007 and the fall of 2010. In September 2008, I contacted the executive director of a southern state's office of People First, a statewide self-advocacy organization run by and for people with disabilities. The executive director, Arlene, gave me permission to attend local chapter meetings, and I volunteered in the office between the fall of 2008 and the spring of 2010.[98] People First is one of the oldest and most well-known self-advocacy groups in the United States. Because the history of exclusion is often cloaked in paternalism, self-advocates are especially skeptical of the ability of nondisabled people to speak for them and are concerned that their movement may be easily co-opted by professionals or parents.[99] Through these observations, I came to see the limitations of my sibling perspective.

More broadly, this project takes from autoethnography a methodological openness to creativity. An ethic of creativity leaves open the possibility that we need new modes of storytelling and theorizing to confront the theoretical puzzles surrounding intellectual disability. Researchers studying people with intellectual disabilities make creative methodological choices in regard to how data are gathered and shared. Jo Aldridge includes intellectually disabled persons in her research by giving them cameras to document their daily obstacles through film.[100] Michael Angrosino presents his ethnography of a residential house for intellectually disabled men as a series of fictional stories to protect the confidentiality of his research subjects.[101] These examples testify to the creative choices that researchers make to respect the integrity of people with intellectual disabilities. In the next section, I review how these tools hammer out the individual chapters of the book.

Conclusion

Because the exclusion of people with intellectual disabilities is entrenched in scholarship, societal attitudes, and the self-advocacy movement itself, this book takes aim at multiple targets, including theoretical texts, historical practices, and current political movements. By asking how political theorists entangle democratic ideals with intellectual disability, this project aims to demonstrate how narratives around citizenship co-construct intellectually disabled *and* nondisabled subjects.

In chapter 1, I argue that anxieties about individual and collective cognitive capacities underwrite our seeming trust in democratic judgment.

I explore the work of John Locke because he entrusts people with political judgment, at the same time writing extensively about persistent errors in men's judgment. Locke also serves as a rich resource, as he is significant to liberal theories of personhood and helped position idiocy as a central category of Enlightenment interest. Locke gives us two sides of the capacity contract—it expands political membership by staking it on equal cognitive faculties, at the same time that it uses cognitive capacity as a way to enforce exclusion. Examining Locke thus helps us see why threshold questions are problematic, as he exploited the indeterminacy of idiocy to stabilize men's rational capacities. Rather than ask if a person is sufficiently able to be a citizen, Locke's legacy prompts us to ask the following questions: What kinds of cognitive mishaps are we vulnerable to? How can we hold the ideal of self-governance without requiring self-sovereignty?

How does Locke's treatment of idiocy and his anxiety about political judgment evolve? Chapter 2 explores the construction of intellectual disabilities; the policies that have surrounded those who have them; and the intersection of disability with race, class, gender, sex, and primates. The histories that I map in this chapter occur primarily between the eighteenth and the twentieth century in France, Britain, and the United States. These approaches share Locke's anxiety about the risks posed to self-governance by cognitive vulnerability, but in contrast to Locke, physicians center this anxiety on the idiot figure. Indeed, they use anxiety as a way to raise collective concern about idiocy, to garner public resources, and to ground their nascent field's legitimacy. For medical professionals, the capacity contract is a way to establish their legitimacy as they take it upon themselves to measure the populace's failure to live up to the demands of compulsory capacity, to rehabilitate some into conformity with the contract, and to hide those who cannot. The second half of the chapter uses this historical analysis to reflect on current critical contract theories that similarly explore histories to map intersecting dimensions of the sexual and racial contracts. We see how the capacity contract works within the racial and sexual contract, as a way to both legitimize oppression and demand recognition for equality.

Chapter 3 shows that the contemporary answer to this anxiety is to disavow the presence of profound intellectual disability as a problem for democratic politics. I explore this disavowal in the work of John Rawls and his critics. The ideal dimension of Rawls's social contract theory forces him to enact a double disavowal of disability: he constructs personhood by denying the full human status of mentally disabled lives and then, by depoliticizing disability, disavows the epistemological function disability actually plays in the formation of his theory. Rawls's work shows us the ways in which idealized cognitive capacities morph into "normal" capacities—a move that naturalizes a fictional account of compulsory capacity, a concept informed by queer and disability studies scholars' work. In the second part of the chapter, I draw on the work of critical and feminist scholars to show how they too hinge emancipatory politics on compulsory capacity. My analysis reveals our entrenched anxiety—for both the world around us and ourselves—from which the double disavowal of disability was designed to protect us.

How do we confront this anxiety without emboldening it? Chapter 4 returns to the self-advocacy meeting in November 2008, where I first met Charles, to explore the evening in more detail and offer an account of politics detached from norms of cognitive capacity. After reviewing the history of the self-advocacy movement, I draw on the work of Hannah Arendt to theorize a kind of empowerment accessible to self-advocates with a range of intellectual disabilities. The ability to act spontaneously in public is a form of political freedom often denied to people with intellectual disabilities. To see the political charge of spontaneous collective action, I compare this November evening to other advocacy events I observed in which people with intellectual disabilities were outnumbered or absent.

Chapter 5, my concluding chapter, explores the 2010 national self-advocacy meeting of SABE (Self Advocates Becoming Empowered) as a way to find specific strategies for tackling anxiety. I detail three methods: alliance, humor, and dance. First, alliance builds on care ethicists' understanding of interdependency, arguing that the success of the self-advocacy movement requires abled and disabled people to mobilize together across anxiety, even amid uneasy partnerships. Second, self-advocates often challenge able-bodied anxieties through humor, whether laughing at ableist fears or revealing the inabilities of the able minded. Humor not only reveals and suspends anxiety but also provides advocates with a sustaining attitude of how to live within anxiety. Finally, dance counters anxiety, as it offers a powerful testament to the positive life experiences of people with intellectual disabilities. I connect these tools to my own experience of being a sibling to a person with autism, as they capture important aspects of our relationship. Alliance, humor, and dance are not new foundations of citizenship; rather, they are democratic modes of action. Thus, an important aim of our work should be to find ways of promoting democratic spaces for action as a way to ensure vibrant contestation of norms and exclusions. In this terrain, anxiety is often an outcome of confrontations of difference that, if persistent, threatens to stifle politics. But if turned on itself, anxiety can crack the rigidity of norms from which it arises.

These tools—alliance, humor, and dance—pose risks and no definitive answers. In contrast, foundational definitions of citizenship offer us (false) promises of the apolitical and the resolute. For many of us who love people with intellectual disabilities, we may yearn for a foundation of solidity from which the people we love can no longer be abused. Foundations of personhood are a seductive promise, and democratic action is risky. Public confrontations with disability may not always dissipate anxiety; in fact, they may even heighten it. But it seems that we cannot move forward without moving in and with risk. Self-advocates give us tools of sustenance: alliance, humor, and dance. These are not only political tools of progress but also political tools of endurance.

What does my formulation of democratic anxiety tell us about issues beyond disability? It says that democratic theorists have more work to do, exposing the funky interplay of human interaction rather than foundational searches for closure. The message is not to end anxiety but to find ways to move, live, speak, and love within it. This is what disability can tell democracy if we can pause and listen to what the sound and the fury signify.

CHAPTER 1

Locke's Capacity Contract and the Construction of Idiocy

I N THE 2013 NPR SERIES *Unfit for Work: The Startling Rise of Disability in America,* Chana Joffe-Walt reported that one in four Americans in Hale County, Alabama, receive assistance through federal disability programs.[1] The "startling" percentage sparked disagreement. Some used it to prove that federal disability programs are awash with former welfare recipients scamming their way onto disability,[2] whereas others argued that NPR missed the bigger picture about the ways in which economic downturns produce disability.[3] What is clear from the story is the contested identity of disability itself: How do we measure disability? Who is disabled? And how can we be sure?

Amid the difficulty determining disability status, political theorists have paid less attention to disability in comparison to other identity groups. Beyond the high number of disabled Americans—18 percent of the population—Nancy Hirschmann argues that there are "epistemological reasons" why we should examine the construction of disability more closely.[4] Disability challenges us to reconsider the cohesion of identity politics amid profound individual variation—from heart disease to autism—and how political alliances are maintained across these differences.

Within the subfield of political theory, John Rawls's political exclusion of people with disabilities—as outliers of human functioning external to the main questions of justice—largely informs the field's uptake of disability.[5] Although theorists often disagree with Rawls's exclusion of disability, they generally agree that people with disabilities constitute a novel category under consideration, as if earlier philosophers overlooked the political dilemma that disability posed to their theories.[6] True, people with disabilities have appeared in political theory as an oppressed category only recently.[7] I take up Rawls's approach to disability in chapter 3; in this chapter, I suggest that the significance of disability to political theory long predates Rawls's foray into the field. Indeed, because so much of political theory premises political inclusion on human capacity, we should expect disability to have been part of the conversation about political subjectivity *all along,* even before political theory took up the question of identity politics.

In fact, John Locke's work repeatedly returns to disability to help specify the relationship between human faculties and political membership. Analyzing Locke not only offers us insight into the construction of disability but also shows us how the constellation of disability and anxiety predates the opening story about Hale County, Alabama. Locke's anxiety centered on the capacities of all men.[8] He recorded the harmful effects of prejudice, custom, ignorance, and lazy thinking all around him, even as he maintained the principle of self-governance—enabling men to judge, consent, and perhaps rebel unwisely.

Across Locke's work, he founds political power on men's rational faculties even as he worries that men seldom employ or consult these faculties. Readers familiar with Locke's *Second Treatise* will recall that human reason is fundamental to his political theory. "There being nothing more evident," according to Locke, "than that creatures of the same species and rank, promiscuously born to all the same advantages of nature, and the use of the same faculties, should also be equal one amongst another without subordination or subjection."[9] Less well known is Locke's explanation of human faculties in *An Essay Concerning Human Understanding,* wherein he explores the prevalence of deficient and unequal faculties, extending upward to the perfect intelligence of angels and downward to the entirely deficient idiot.[10]

The idiot appears often in Locke's writing, and idiocy plays a key role for him in defining the meaning of personhood and limiting political membership. Whereas Locke draws on sensory, physical, and emotional disabilities to help define key concepts, his treatment of intellectual disability—or idiocy, as he calls it—plays a distinct role because of the importance he gives to rationality. Idiots appear in Locke's earliest political writings, *Two Tracts on Government* and *Essays on the Law of Nature,* and in his most significant publications, *An Essay Concerning Human Understanding* (henceforth *Essay*) and *Two Treatises of Government.* In Locke's *Essay,* he uses idiots to disprove the maxim of innate ideas and test the limits of species membership, and in the *Second Treatise*, he excludes idiots from political membership.

Despite disability's constant circulation in Locke's thought, few scholars focus on his treatment of disability—or, more specifically, his construction and political exclusion of the idiot. When political philosophers examine Locke's treatment of disability, they tend to discuss it as a small part of a larger analysis—for instance, commenting on the history of disability in Western political thought, the limits of Lockean equality, or the idiot's role in confounding Aristotelian notions of species.[11] Although disability studies scholars have described how Locke influenced the medicalization of intellectual disability, they focus less on linking Locke's account of disability to his political theory.[12]

Understanding Locke's treatment of disability provides a new way to read his social contract as a *capacity contract*, which bases political membership on a threshold level of capacity and excludes anyone who falls below. My interpretation is consistent with critical social contract scholarship, pioneered by Carole Pateman's sexual contract and Charles Mills's racial contract, both of which unmask contractual equality as a ruse for domination.[13] As Brooke Ackerly argues, domination contracts are social contracts "*among some people with certain power* about which people or categories of people are 'persons' in the sense of being cognitive equals."[14] By excluding anyone with deficient reasoning capacity from the social compact, Locke attempts to expel the anxiety over insufficient cognitive capacity. Whereas Locke's capacity contract is a domination contract—by privileging the more over the less able—my analysis shows how domination contracts *are* capacity contracts: political exclusion is justified on the supposed deficient capacities of women, nonwhites, and the less powerful.

Yet Locke's work on disability reveals another and more emancipatory side of the capacity contract—a side that sees vulnerability as an essential marker of human life that prompts men to form and maintain the social compact amid personal incapacity. Rather than answer incapacity with anxiety and exclusion, this side of the contract responds with solidarity. My reading of the capacity contract as a *solidarity contract* follows from Christine Keating's work on the postcolonial sexual contract and its ability to promote both exclusion and solidarity.[15] Although Susan Burgess and Keating acknowledge the social contract's proclivity toward domination, they also encourage us to reinvent a more participatory and democratic contract.[16] As I will show, Locke helps us see how disability helps build solidarity in his *Second Treatise* and contemporary politics.

My analysis of disability gives us new ways to see Locke's contract and, in addition, helps explain his treatment of an assortment of marginalized groups—savages, women, mad men, the physically impaired—who are stigmatized because of their diminished human faculties but not irreconcilable to human experience. As Hirschmann points out, these deficiencies are due to the imperfect training and exercise of reason.[17] Their location, even if marginal, is a difference of degree, not category. Idiots—and others who similarly lack the faculty of thinking—shift imprecisely between humans and beasts. Understanding idiots' twofold relationship to vulnerability—both on a continuum of vulnerability and below a threshold—will pull Locke's contract in opposing directions of domination and democratic solidarity, a struggle that continues to impede significant change for people with disabilities today.

Idiocy in Seventeenth-Century England

To understand Locke's depiction of idiocy in the *Essay,* this section paints in broad brushstrokes the cultural landscape of idiocy in which Locke was located. Constructing a coherent narrative, however, is difficult. Definitions of idiocy in the seventeenth century ranged from the uneducated to private persons to the incurably dull.[18] Etymologically, *idiot* derives from the Greek *idiotis,* meaning "private person, common man, plebeian, [or] one without professional knowledge."[19] Other terms used in seventeenth-century England included *innocents, stupid, dolts, naturals, fools,* and *natural fools.* Although similar in meaning, these terms can encompass different kinds of people, as we see by contrasting Hobbes's "Foole" with Locke's idiot. In the *Leviathan,* the fool deceptively enters contracts, whereas Locke's idiot cannot form abstract ideas and seldom speaks.[20] As this section shows, the meaning of idiocy was in flux, due to changes in legal, religious, and medical thinking.

During medieval England, fools—a category that could encompass natural fools and artificial fools—entertained nobles.[21] According to Sandra Billington, "kings and nobility frequently kept simpleton fools to remind themselves of their own morality and imperfections."[22] It was a popular joke at the time "to say that the state of King and Fool were the only ones to which you had to be born and could not otherwise attain."[23] Some of the most well-known royal entertainers were artificial fools—people who feigned ignorance so that their insubordinate witticism would go unpunished. Will Somers (an artificial fool) and Patch (a natural fool) both entertained Henry VIII, and fools continued to perform into the reign of Charles I.[24]

Despite their popularity, fools and "lunatics" faced harsh legal and institutional exclusions. Because idiocy was considered a permanent condition, according to Richard Neugebauer, "any rents and profits collected by the Crown during the idiocy, in excess of costs of the individual's upkeep, were considered a legitimate source of royal revenue."[25] In contrast, because people could recover from madness, accumulated wealth reverted to recovered lunatics or to their heirs. To determine whether someone was an idiot or a lunatic, a group of twelve or more men would participate in trial-like procedures referred to as "inquisitions," and both men and women were subject to competency hearings. Men judged an individual for knowledge of his own name, age, and kin; simple arithmetic and literacy skills; and whether his personal appearance resembled the "countenance of an idiot."[26] Between 1540 and 1660 in England and Wales, a single Court of Wards and Liveries determined competence, created in part to deter the exploitation of idiots by unsound guardians.[27]

Using curability as the marker between madness and idiots continued to be important in English society, as demonstrated in the seventeenth-century legal writings of Sir Edward Coke. Coke described the legal culpability of the different categories of *non compos mentis*, including idiots, lunatics, and drunkards. According to Coke, the idiot "is known by his perpetual infirmity of natura, a *nativate*, for he never had any sense or understanding to contract with any man." Because the idiot is incurable, he cannot "defend or govern himself," and all of his belongings and his body belong to the king.[28]

Beginning in the seventeenth century, religious debates regarding the soul led to the shifting spiritual status of idiots, which in turn influenced their political status.[29] Early English opinion considered fools closer to God, presuming that their mental deficiency left them incapable of deceit and thus absolved from sin.[30] This spiritual innocence extended civilly, as we see in court fools whose insubordination to kings was both comic and beyond blame. As Protestants moved away from a belief in Calvinist predestination, however, individual comprehension of God became essential for personal salvation. According to C. F. Goodey, this new theology endangered the souls of idiots unaware of God, which then intensified the superstitious belief in idiocy's satanic origin.[31]

Concurrent with religious upheavals, scientific studies of the mind and body also incriminated idiots. For example, Sarah Cohen argues that anatomical studies showing the similarity between human and non-human bodies placed fresh emphasis on philosophers to distinguish the unique specificity of the human soul. Descartes takes up this challenge in his *Discourse on the Method* in 1637. According to Cohen, "For Descartes it was precisely through comparison of human to animal that one could perceive the spiritual distinctiveness of human soul, the spiritual being understood as *fundamentally intellectual* and the seat of human reason."[32] For Cohen, Descartes's answer failed to resolve the difference between the souls of humans and animals, but it also left unanswered the condition of humans bereft of reason.

Idiocy also attracted the attention of Thomas Willis—a medical contemporary of Locke—who was among the first to promote the educability of idiots. Inspired by work with deaf pupils, Willis argued that mental deficiency, while not curable, was amenable to medical and educational interventions that could restore basic elements of learning. He designated two categories of idiocy—stupidity and fools—the latter of which was less severe. Willis's belief that idiocy could have multiple causes—including heredity, drunkenness, illness, and severe injury—was unique for his time.[33] Though Locke was a student of Willis's, he disregarded his typology of stupidity and fools, and rejected Willis's belief in the educability of idiots.[34]

To summarize, in seventeenth-century England, the meaning and significance of idiocy was evolving in religious, medical, and political spheres. Locke's *Essay,* published in 1689, took advantage of idiocy's indeterminate boundaries, both building on and disregarding prevalent strains in conventional opinion. The shape-shifting quality of Locke's idiot—as both within and beyond human membership—gives his social compact in the *Second Treatise* the elasticity to both enforce exclusion and build solidarity on the basis of vulnerability.

Disability and Vulnerability in Locke's *Essay*

By analyzing Locke's treatment of disability in the *Essay* in order to interpret his social compact in the *Second Treatise*, I am treading on a well-worn path of scholarship that debates the precise relationship between these two texts, which were published in the same year, albeit the latter anonymously. For John Dunn, these texts present an irresolvable tension, as Locke never demonstrates in the *Essay* how men come to know the law of reason even while the *Second Treatise* assumes all men can access reason equally.[35] Others, like Peter Laslett, argue that squaring these texts is mistaken, as they were "written for an entirely different purpose and in an entirely different state of mind."[36] In contrast, Jeremy Waldron reads the *Second Treatise* with the *Essay* to argue that Locke grounds political authority in the "ordinary intellect" of everyday people, including the poor and uneducated.[37] Yet other scholars argue that Locke exploits differences in rationality to sanction political domination, particularly toward the poor, women, the insane, savages, and criminals.[38] I suggest that tensions between the *Essay* and the *Second Treatise* may be most productive when they remain unresolved: that Locke emphasizes men's shared vulnerability when he needs to promote democratic solidarity and draws on differences in men's faculties when he needs to justify political exclusion.

The main task of Locke's *Essay* is to determine the limits of human understanding, and disability plays a prominent role in symbolizing common defects.[39] Locke breaks with traditional opinion that locates morality in innate ideas, instead arguing that human understanding derives from experience. He divides human faculties into two categories—sensation and reflection—and he uses different corporeal defects to signify human limits in both. Locke's close attention to human frailties perhaps arises from his medical training detailing various ailments and remedies.[40] Regardless, Locke exploits corporeal defects like blindness, deafness, madness, paralysis, and idiocy to help characterize common defects in human understanding. For Locke, corporeality makes all men defective in relation to God, but when these defects are so severe as to annihilate faculties of perception, men resemble lower forms of life on the great chain of being.[41]

Blindness captures well Locke's ability to exploit the symbolic value of corporeal defects. Locke uses blindness to represent the absurdity of innate ideas, the inability to know real essences, the consequences of lazy thinking, and universal human vulnerability in relation to God. Locke encourages "any one try to fancy any Taste, which had never affected his Palate; or frame the *Idea* of a Scent he had never smelt: And when he can do this, I will also conclude that a blind man hath *Ideas* of Colours, and a deaf Man true distinct Notions of Sounds" (*Essay*, 2.2.2).[42] Locke uses the same rationale—that a blind man can know the color of pansies—to attack scholastic attempts to determine species' real essences (4.6.5). Locke also argues that blindness is analogous to impaired or inattentive senses within nondisabled bodies. Whereas "it is impossible for a blind man . . . to read a legal notice displayed in a public place," it is similarly "difficult for one who sees badly."[43] Finally, when Locke describes men living in a "fleeting state of Action and Blindness," he means to capture all men, not just the blind, in relationship to God's perfect intelligence (4.16.4; 2.21.50). In this way, Locke uses blindness to symbolize men's shared vulnerability.

Similarly, Locke turns to physical defects to symbolize corporeal unruliness and to explore the meaning of liberty for all men. In the chapter "On Power," Locke describes a man who involuntarily hits himself due to a "convulsive motion" and another man with palsy whose legs are incapable of "obeying the determination of his Mind" (2.21.11). For Locke, "so far as a Man has a power to think, or not to think; to move, or not to move, according to the preference or direction of his own mind, so far is a Man *Free*" (2.21.8). Accordingly, for these paralytic bodies, Locke argues, "nobody thinks he has in this liberty: everyone pities him as acting by necessity and constraint" (2.21.9). Yet Locke argues that the paralytic is capable of liberty: whenever he prefers to be stationary rather than in motion, his motionlessness is voluntary (2.21.11). Additionally, Locke encourages readers to consider moments of bodily unruliness within "our own bodies," most evident in the fact that no man can control the beating of his heart (2.21.11). Locke thus treats sensory and physical disabilities on a continuum of human capacities that limit understanding and freedom but fail to detract from human standing altogether.

When Locke considers defects in the faculties of perception and retention, however, he suggests that men can come to resemble beasts if their defect is severe. Due to their undeveloped or degraded faculty of perception, Locke compares fetuses to vegetables (2.1.21) and the old who have lost their memory to oysters, cockles, and the "lowest degree of Animals" (2.9.14). Rather than residing along a spectrum of human capacities, fetuses and the senile resemble a different category of life form altogether.

This difference in category is due to the importance that Locke places on perception and memory, the latter of which is essential to all other faculties. If memory is "wanting," then "all the rest of our Faculties are in a great measure useless" (2.10.8). Deprived of memory, the mind cannot move from the mere awareness of objects to conceptualizing objects as ideas and hence can never reason. Although memory is essential, Locke acknowledges that no man possesses it perfectly, leaving perfection to God and "some superior created intellectual Beings" only (2.10.9). Locke also describes different levels of defects in men's memory. The dull and stupid have minds that fail to move "quick enough"; hence, they "[lose] the opportunity" for action (2.10.8). The perfectly ignorant man "loses the Idea" instantaneously—so quickly as to have never existed at all (2.10.8).

Defects that impede men's faculty of reason are the most significant because reason is the faculty most vital to Locke's definition of personhood. According to Locke, birth does not bestow species membership. Instead, the faculty of thinking separates the meaning of man from person. Man, according to Locke, is "nothing but a participation of the same continued life . . . united to the same organized body" (2.27.6). A person, however, "is a thinking intelligent being, that has reason and reflection, and can consider it self as it self" (2.27.9). Locke stresses the dependence of personhood on consciousness, arguing that "without consciousness, there is no Person" (2.27.23) and, again, "Self is that conscious thinking thing" (2.27.17; 2.27.9). Limitations in sensation or perception impede human understanding, but defects that annihilate reasoning faculties fall outside Locke's definition of personhood.

Locke uses several figures throughout the *Essay* to explore the absence of reason—fetuses, the old, and changelings—but he returns most often to the idiot, across all four books of the *Essay*. Despite idiocy's prominence, its precise deficiency is difficult to determine, as the idiot's defect shifts according to its surrounding cast of characters and whichever task Locke has at hand.[44] When Locke aims at the main task of the *Essay*—to discern the limits of human understanding—he places idiots next to the defects of all men, as they all fall short of God's perfect intelligence. Occasionally, however, when Locke challenges the coherence of species, we find idiots alongside changelings, as well as drills, dogs, hogs, and horses (3.6.41, 3.6.12).[45] Locke thus describes cognitive deficiency both as a universal continuum along which all men are fallible and as a threshold under which some men fall.

Idiocy and Rationality

When Locke first introduces the idiot in book one of the *Essay*, he uses the idiot to help dismantle the maxim of innate ideas. If innate maxims exist, Locke suggests that we should find them in "Children, Ideots, Savages, and Illiterate People" (1.3.27). Locke concludes, however, "'tis evident that all *Children* and *Ideots* have not the least Apprehension or Thought of them" (1.2.5). Although a child recognizes his nurse and the savage loves hunting, Locke finds no impression "on the Minds of *Naturals*" (1.3.27). Locke depicts the capacity for understanding both in terms of degree—for instance, with infants, children, and savages—and as a sharp dichotomy between idiots who cannot learn and all others who can.

Locke attributes the idiot's absence of ideas to an internal defect, making the idiot corporeally different from other men. In *Essays on the Law of Nature,* Locke writes:

> If this law of nature were written in our hearts, why do the foolish and insane have no knowledge of it, since the law is said to be stamped immediately on the soul itself and this depends very little upon the constitution and structure of the body's organs? Yet therein admittedly lies the only difference between the wise and the stupid.[46]

In the *Essay,* Locke similarly argues that the "Organs of the Body" are "the only confessed difference between [Naturals] and others" (1.2.27). Importantly, Locke's indictment of the body's organs signals permanent bodily difference between idiots and other men. Unlike children who learn the law of nature, idiocy is forever.

Men can come to resemble idiots, however, and this is a point Locke often strikes to castigate the ill results of indolence among men without corporeal defects. Locke speculates into the "great difference in men's intellects, whether it rises from any defect in the Organs of the Body particularly adapted to Thinking; or in the dulness or untractableness of those Faculties, for want of use" (4.20.5). In *Essays on the Law of Nature*, Locke distinguishes between the dull "who make no use of the light of reason but prefer darkness" and those for whom "through natural defect the acumen of the mind is too dull to be able to bring to light those secret decrees of nature."[47] In these passages, Locke uses the distinction between bodily difference and indolence to disparage most men, not idiots, because only the former merit blame for their failure to use their reasoning ability. In order for Locke's disparagement to work, however, it must hinge on the lower status of idiots, a likeness most men would want to reject.

This bodily difference affects idiots' standing, as they occupy an indeterminate space between mad men and beasts. In book two, Locke offers a history of human knowledge, arranged from brutes to idiots to mad men—a chronology that proceeds from the absence of abstraction to the excesses of it. In the beginning, "brutes come far short of men" (2.11.7). Because brutes can compare simple ideas—albeit in a very limited fashion—Locke maintains that they can reason. However, they lack the faculty of abstraction, which, for Locke, is why "the Species of *Brutes* are discriminated from Man" (2.11.11). Although the inability to abstract separates brutes from man, Locke's depiction of reasoning faculties on a continuum blurs species' boundaries.

Idiots, who represent the historical period between brutes and mad men, further blur this boundary, as their deficiencies closely replicate brutish capacities. Idiots "cannot distinguish, compare, and abstract, would hardly be able to understand and make use of Language, or judge or reason to any tolerable degree" (2.11.12). For Locke, "the defect in *Naturals* seems to proceed from want of quickness, activity, and motion, in the intellectual Faculties, whereby they are *deprived* of Reason" (2.11.13, emphasis added). Locke speculates that, like brutes, if idiots can reason, it is minimal only and derived directly from what is most familiar to their senses. At the same time, however, Locke states that idiots are "deprived" of reason, seemingly placing them below the capacities of brutes.

In contrast, Locke sharply distinguishes between idiots and mad men, as idiots symbolize reason's absence whereas mad men constitute reason's excess. According to Locke, "mad Men put wrong *Ideas* together, and so make wrong Propositions, but argue and reason right from them: But Idiots make very few or no Propositions, and reason scarce at all" (2.11.13). Locke continues his chronology, comparing a "very sober" man to a mad man, as a sober man can seem mad from undue obsession (2.11.13). Just as men resemble idiots in their indolence or the blind in their inexperience, so too can passion make men seem mad.[48]

Locke's "true History on the first beginnings of Human Knowledge" illustrates how idiocy's defect remains indeterminate. When he introduces the idiot in his chronology, Locke states, "How far *Idiots* are concerned in the want of weakness of any, or all of the foregoing Faculties, an exact observation of their several ways of faltering, would no doubt discover" (2.11.12). Locke leaves open the question of whether idiots have faulty or absent faculties, a difference he states we could discover, but which he seems disinclined to pursue. Moreover, shortly after stating that idiots are deprived of reason, Locke suggests that there are "degrees of Madness, as of Folly" (2.11.13). If there are degrees of folly, then it seems that the difference between brutes, idiots, and rational men is incremental, not categorical. Like other corporeal defects, Locke locates idiocy along a continuum of capacities and, at the same time, as the absence of reasoning capacity.

Indeed, in book four, Locke assigns changelings—*not* idiots—to a status "something between Man and Beast." In the seventeenth century, a changeling was defined as a "half-witted person, idiot, [and] imbecile," as well as a "child (usually stupid or ugly) supposed to have been left by fairies in exchange for one stolen child."[49] Scholars contest the precise difference between the idiot and the changeling. For John Yolton and Christopher Hughes Conn, Locke's changelings are synonymous with idiots, whereas Anthony Krupp argues that changelings are "neither persons nor human."[50] C. F. Goodey and Tim Stainton argue that Locke defines idiots and changelings differently.[51] But elsewhere Goodey suggests that Locke's changeling *is* an "'idiot' infant born to normal parents."[52] I suggest both sides are right. Locke exploits the indeterminacy between changelings and idiots, as their ignorance exemplifies the universal limits of human understanding *and* the outer limits of what is recognizably human.

Locke uses changelings to debunk two misplaced assumptions: "That all Things that have the outward Shape and Appearance of a Man, must necessarily be designed to an immortal future Being, after this Life. Or, secondly, that whatever is of humane Birth, must be so"

(4.4.15).[53] Locke describes changelings as "drivelling, unintelligent, [and] intractable," "half Beast, and half Man," and "ill-formed and misshaped productions" (4.4.16). Locke asks, "Shall a defect in the Body make a *Monster;* a defect in the Mind, (the far more Noble and, in the common phrase, the far more Essential Part), not?" (4.4.16) Locke dismisses outward corporeal defects as threats to personhood (2.27.17), ridiculing the idea that "the external Shape of his Body" could determine the "Excellency of a Man" (4.4.15), and thus chastises the killing of infants based on physical defect (3.6.26). In contrast,

we should find that the *Idea* of the Shape, Motion, and Life of a Man without Reason, is as much a distinct *Idea,* and makes as much a distinct sort of Things from Man and Beast, as the *Idea* of the Shape of an *Ass* with Reason, would be different from either that of Man or Beast, and be a Species of an Animal between, or distinct from both. (4.4.13)

Hence, changelings "are something between a Man and Beast" (4.4.13). Assigning a soul to a changeling because of its human shape is like seeing souls in statues (4.4.15).

What is the relationship between changelings and idiots for Locke? Both are deficient in reason, and earlier in the *Essay,* Locke uses "naturals" and "changelings" interchangeably, as both question the stability and essential markers of the human species. In regard to naturals, "There are Creatures in the World, that have shapes like ours, but are hairy, and want Language, and Reason. There are Naturals amongst us, that have perfectly our shape, but want Reason, and some of them Language too" (3.6.22). Similarly, Locke asks,

Shall not the difference of Hair only on the Skin, be a mark of a different internal specific Constitution between a Changeling and a Drill, when they agree in Shape, and want of Reason, and Speech? And shall not the want of Reason and Speech, be a sign to us of different real Constitutions and *Species,* between a Changeling, and a reasonable Man? (3.6.22)

These passages speak both to the importance of reason as a requirement for species membership and to the strong resemblance among changelings, naturals, and brutes.

When Locke questions the spiritual standing of changelings, he again leaves the answer indeterminate. For Locke, human status hinges on reason, because reason is "that faculty which comes nearest the excellency of [God's] own incomprehensible being" (2.1.15). Locke asks, "If *Changelings* are something between Man and Beast, what will become of them in the other World?" (4.4.14). Like his description of idiots in his history of human knowledge, Locke answers, "It concerns me not to know or enquire" (4.4.14). Locke elaborates, however, that all those "capable of Instruction, Discourse, and Reasoning" must answer to God, seemingly excluding both changelings and idiots from the kingdom of heaven (4.4.14). Exclusion from heaven carries with it exclusion from politics as well, as men who cannot know the law of nature can never be subject to it.

Epistemological Uncertainty

The idiot's indeterminate human and spiritual status infused the larger cultural context of disability in seventeenth-century England, as definitions of idiocy were in flux, but there are also reasons internal to Locke's project that help us understand the idiot's ambiguity. Part of this indeterminacy derives from the idiot's partial materialization throughout Locke's text. Because Locke's method of understanding requires consulting experience before entering judgment, he often details different ways of life and records anecdotes of subaltern identities. For instance, Locke recounts Garcilaso de la Vega's depiction of American Indians contracting with the Swiss;[54] Gilles Ménage's story of the deformed birth of the Abbot of St. Martin (3.6.26); Prince Maurice's tale of a talking parrot (2.27.8); a mad man who thought his body was made of glass (2.11.13); and "some *Changelings,* who have lived forty years together" (4.4.13). In contrast, he never refers to any particular idiot. On the one hand, this absence is surprising, given Locke's empirical method of consulting experience and the detailing of other marginalized identities. On the other hand, this absence is essential. When defined as the absence of thought, the idiot for Locke has no identity—by his own definition of personal identity. But if degrees of idiocy exist, then Locke cannot risk an example lest the idiot too closely resemble the majority of faulty and irrational men—men he grants political membership.

Idiocy's shape-shifting quality also results from Locke's depiction of human corporeality as itself indeterminate. In the *Essay*, Locke states, "An Accident, or Disease may very much alter my Colour, or Shape; a Fever, or Fall, may take away my Reason, or Memory, or both; and an Apoplexy leave neither Sense, nor Understanding, no nor Life" (3.6.4). Indeed, Locke draws on imaginative and implausible situations, as well as mundane features of everyday life, to question the boundaries of personal identity in the *Essay*. Locke gives the example of the wrongfulness of punishing a sleeping Socrates for what the waking Socrates committed, as this would be like punishing "one Twin for what his Brother-Twin did, whereof he knew nothing, because their outsides were so like, that they could not be distinguished" (2.27.19). Locke also offers the possibility of a finger cut from the body of a man wherein the consciousness follows the finger rather than the body. The finger, possessing consciousness, remains a person.

This indeterminacy, which is internal to a man's own body, spreads to describe men's relationship to other men and nonhuman animals. "Other Creatures of my shape, may be made with more, and better, or fewer and worse Faculties than I have: and others may have Reason, and Sense, in a shape and body very different from mine" (3.6.4). Locke heightens this sense of individual indeterminacy by situating it within a world "in so constant a flux."[55] The idiot's corporeal defect may be distinct, but corporeality is by nature indeterminate.

The indeterminacy of men's faculties has political consequences for Locke, particularly in regard to legal judgment, and he uses the example of crimes committed while intoxicated to question the culpability of men. Locke maintains that magistrates are legitimate to hold drunkards responsible for their actions because "want of consciousness cannot be proved."[56] Here Locke suggests that proving consciousness is impossible. In the case of the drunk who has committed a crime, it is well to assume him sober, for it cannot be proven that he was unconscious of the crimes he did commit.

Finally, insofar as Locke's epistemology recognizes human limits in understanding, it allows him to leave some of the world's knowledge beyond men's control—a point to which his *Essay* repeatedly returns. These limits directly impinge on the status of idiots, as Locke states, "'Tis an hard Matter to say where Sensible and Rational begin, and where Insensible and Irrational end: and who is there quick-sighted enough to determine precisely, which is the lowest Species of living Things, and which the first of those which have no Life?" (4.16.12). Locke's religious beliefs accord this task to God only. Species' boundaries are "unknown and undetermined" (4.6.4), arising in part from the invisible maneuvering of the mind (2.1.19). Epistemological uncertainty should prevent men from making absolute distinctions between men as well as within men, but this uncertainty jeopardizes political judgment, forcing men to forfeit epistemological humility in exchange for political expediency—as the case of the accused drunken criminal exposes. Rereading Locke's social contract in light of this epistemological indeterminacy offers us a new way to interpret its foundation.

The Capacity Contract

Like the *Essay,* the *Second Treatise* is a story about capacities, as Locke's oft-repeated question, *who shall judge,* asks who has the capacities of judgment.[57] Capacity is central to Locke's theory of equality, as "Creatures of the same species and rank . . . , and the use of the same faculties, should also be equal one amongst another without Subordination or Subjection."[58] Superior faculties give men power over "inferior ranks of Creatures," and anyone failing to pass this threshold suffers political exclusion.[59] Locke's focus on capacity allows us to see how his social contract is a capacity contract: only individuals who pass a threshold level of cognitive capacity can consent and therefore merit political membership.

Accordingly, in the chapter "Of Paternal Power," Locke states, "lunatics and idiots are never set free from the government of their parents."[60] Locke's ability to exclude idiots based on permanent and corporeal defect helps bolster the rational capacities and political standing of other men. While exclusion based on insufficient capacities is one face of domination within the contract, there is also another. The capacity contract gives men the power to measure one another. By resting political membership on a threshold level of rational capacity, Locke's contract empowers some men with the examination and removal of defective others.[61]

Scholars, however, find Locke's exclusion of idiots unproblematic, in part because Locke accords idiots charity, but I believe what is more important is most scholars' complicity with Locke's capacity contract, as they agree that political membership requires a threshold level of cognitive capacity.[62] Indeed, many scholars interpret Locke's grant of equal capacities broadly, arguing that it covers most men[63] or that it can encompass all people through education, such as the form of educational instruction that Locke proscribes in *Some Thoughts Concerning Education* and *The Conduct of the Understanding*.[64] Thus, Button describes the "transformative ethos" embedded in Locke's contract, as its purpose is to shape men into citizens, thus making the contract into a tool of cognitive metamorphosis.[65] Even scholars who criticize Locke for his political exclusions often do so on terms that comply with the capacity contract, arguing that Locke *falsely* attributes inferior capacities to women, nonwhites, and the poor rather than contending that incapacity is an unfair justification for political exclusion.[66]

Despite Locke's clear exclusion of idiots and lunatics from the contract, he also describes certain moments in which human incapacity prompts men to form and maintain the contract. Moreover, this vulnerability persists, as men remain inattentive and ignorant after forming the social compact. Importantly, this alternate capacity contract aims at solidarity, not cognitive transformation. Men's vulnerability—both physical and cognitive—prompts men to form a solidarity capacity contract, ensuring that all men can appeal to justice.

Prior to the contract moment, Locke describes how cognitive and physical vulnerability can lead to injustice. The first, and more analyzed, occurs between thieves and innocents as the aftermath of crime threatens to blur the boundary of criminality. Enraged by their victimization, innocent men become bloodthirsty, vindictive, and blind to their own bias.[67] Locke avoids the language of cognitive defect in describing vengeance, but he shows us how men who have no judge to appeal to and who must carry out punishment themselves act amid bias and their inability to see their own bias.

The second precontract moment occurs as Locke argues that corporeal vulnerability can leave men unable to protect themselves, which gives men another reason to form a contract. The chapter "On Conquest" describes "Great Robbers," and as Waldron helps us see, much of Locke's use of the robber is an analogy for the corrupt crown. "What is my Remedy against a Robber, that so broke into my House?" asks Locke. "*Appeal* to the Law for Justice. But perhaps Justice is denied, or I am crippled and cannot stir, robbed and have not the means to do it."[68] If the "Great Robbers" are monarchs, unhinged from natural law, then "crippled and cannot stir" equally applies to men living within unjust systems. In this sense, men cannot appeal either because the sovereign has confiscated their "means" of justice or because their own bodies have thwarted their ability to retaliate. Men enter into the contract knowing that they need political solidarity to ensure their ability to appeal to justice even when they are bodily incapable of accessing the means of appeal on their own.

Corporeal vulnerability also surfaces in the contract moment itself. Locke argues that the consent of the majority is sufficient to form a society, refuting the claim that only "the consent of every individual can make any thing to be the act of the whole." Locke states, "such a consent is next to impossible ever to be had, if we consider the Infirmities of Health, and the Avocations of Business."[69] Locke's linkage of infirmities of health and avocations of business suggest that neither condition denies men political standing but that both are temporal problems that prevent men from being publicly present in the contract moment. Locke's reference to infirmities of health is indeterminate, potentially affecting the body or mind. Like the man who has the right but not the means to persecute the robber, men infirm in health do not forfeit their political right—just the political moment.

After the contract, Locke uses cognitive defects to ground stability for political society. Locke responds to arguments that entrusting the people will lead to ruin, as they are "ignorant, and always discontented," with an "unsteady Opinion, and uncertain Humour."[70] Importantly, Locke's response avoids defending the cognitive judgment of men but draws on the influence of habit, stating, "People are not so easily got out of their old Forms." Although Locke elsewhere attacks habit for thwarting reason, he draws on these same habitual proclivities to protect the stability of governance.

Moreover, the vulnerability of men extends to sovereigns, thus bolstering stability in a different direction. For Locke, "*Great mistakes* in the ruling part, many wrong and inconvenient Laws, and all the *slips* of humane frailty will be *born by the People,* without mutiny or murmur."[71] Locke suggests that sovereigns will err not due to malfeasance but due to their own corporeal vulnerability—that these slips are in some ways unavoidable—and that the people understand this, or at least, this humane frailty is part of the backdrop of why revolutions will not easily occur on "every little mismanagement in publick affairs."[72] Locke thus turns the fear of men's ignorance on its head, arguing that it is men's ignorance, inattentiveness, and corporeal limitations that help stabilize government.

These moments in Locke's *Second Treatise* reveal shared vulnerability as the essential binding elements of men's social contract even as his domination capacity contract remains the more robust version. Nevertheless, today's readers can use Locke's insight on vulnerability and epistemological uncertainty to rethink the relationship among capacity, disability, and democratic membership. If we choose to do so, we can draw at least three interlocking conclusions.

First, shared corporeal vulnerability is the condition of politics on which we should focus. Locke's domination contract ignores the full range of human vulnerability, understanding vulnerability primarily in men's relationship to the sovereign, thus narrowing the scope of politics. But if we begin with shared corporeal vulnerability, then we arrive at a broader understanding of politics. Following Joan Tronto, when we focus on shared vulnerability, then "once a democratic society makes a commitment to the equality of all its members, then the ways in which the inequalities of care affect different citizens' capacities to be equal has to be a central part of the society's *political* tasks."[73] Locke's domination contract depoliticizes these questions by excluding vulnerability from the public sphere.

Second, if the basis for the social compact is human vulnerability, then we should reject the domination contract because it bases political solidarity on a false foundation of equal, stable, and measureable capacities. Moreover, the indeterminacy of all men's bodies should make us pause before we too quickly follow Locke's charge of exclusion based on inferior capacity. Recall that it is a "hard Matter to say where Sensible and Rational begin, and where Insensible and Irrational end" (4.16.12), especially as this demarcation similarly divides those who can appeal to justice from the rest. Who would Locke entrust with this judgment? While he grants that "if Men were better instructed themselves, they would be less imposing on others" (4.16.4), he also assumes that most men are too lazy or too busy to pursue rational instruction, and thus unfit to be sovereign over anyone.

Fortunately, Locke's work contains the seeds of how to rework the contract, which leads to the third and final conclusion. In Locke's democratic capacity contract, we as citizens stick together and err on the side of justice for the vulnerable because we are cognizant that we are all vulnerable and limited. Waldron helps us see these new political stakes, even though he takes Locke's emphasis on capacity to draw the borders of responsibility rather than uncertainty:

> When I catch a rabbit, I know that I am not dealing with a
> creature that has the capacity to abstract, and so I know that
> there is no question of this being one of God's special servants,
> sent into the world about his business. But if I catch a human in
> full possession of his faculties, I know I should be careful how
> I deal with him.[74]

Waldron's example of the rabbit follows logically from Locke's domination capacity contract, but it also illustrates why we should find this version of the contract so problematic. To rephrase Waldron's claim, why should I extend the principle of justice or charity to anyone I suspect falls below a threshold level of capacity? And who shall be empowered to draw this boundary? Locke's work on disability, which illustrates how all of us are prone to corporeal vulnerability, along with his epistemological indeterminacy, suggests an alternative way to read this encounter and his social contract.

Specifically, no man is always in full possession of his faculties, and no man can be confident in his own judgment denying another man's consciousness. Moreover, he cannot rely on a mythical social contract moment that transforms his corporeal limitation into cerebral perfection. Therefore, if I cannot know definitively, then I should err on the side of solidarity. Although Locke's domination contract may be the more robust, we can use his theory to help reinvent a more expansive democratic contract.

Conclusion: Defective Democracy?

Understanding Locke's treatment of idiocy gives us insight into how he managed his own anxiety on mixing ignorance with authority. One of the ways in which Locke did so was by describing the corporeal defective idiot figure as permanently empty rather than marred, which served to bolster the rational capacities of most men. In chapter 2, I explore how medical men constructed idiocy, which incorporated much of Locke's understanding of idiocy and education. In contrast to Locke, they argue that idiots are educable and thus worthy of state-endorsed rehabilitation. Medical men also shift Locke's anxiety, moving it away from the broader democratic populace toward defective outsiders.

Another way Locke managed his anxiety—apart from exclusion—was to embrace uncertainty as fundamental to epistemological humility. We can understand this strategy as a democratic capacity contract: individuals build solidarity by creating uncertainty about whose bodies in the public sphere are most vulnerable. The democratic capacity contract aims at troubling the stability of social categories. For Charles Mills, seeing the world as an endless social construction is one of the great advantages of social contract theory.[75] But while Locke's solidarity contract embraces uncertainty as a component of epistemological humility, his domination contract enforces judgment to ensure political expediency. Like the drunk whom we cannot know to be unconscious, we must presume his guilt to ensure justice.

Locke's tension between uncertainty and judgment resonates with the current disability rights movement and the opening story of the "startling rise" of disability in America. On the one hand, disability rights activists use uncertainty to promote solidarity. For example, in *Crip Theory*, Robert McRuer describes how South Africa's Treatment Action Campaign (TAC) used uncertainty about HIV status to build solidarity. The group created T-shirts reading "HIV POSITIVE" both to signal ambiguity about who has HIV and to shift conversations about HIV from an individual's medical status to political solidarity.[76] Similarly, delegates at the United Nations Convention on the Rights of Persons with Disabilities (CRPD) refused to define disability at all.[77] Like TAC, the CRPD is less interested in marking bodies as disabled and more focused on building alliances among all people—with or without disabilities. Rather than try to eliminate uncertainty for political judgment, activists exacerbate it to diminish divisions between people.

Yet uncertainty cannot persist indefinitely due to the ways in which political structures use disability status to determine public benefits. Like the opening example of disability benefits in Hale County, Alabama, people can receive benefits only if the court of law recognizes them as disabled. Here, uncertainty about disability status leads to the denial of disability benefits. Uncertainty thus produces anxiety, as we worry about people "passing" as disabled to escape responsibility. Thus, uncertainty invites closure—a desire to maintain strict categories between the abled and the nondisabled in order to safeguard political judgment. Here, the two sides of Locke's capacity contract pull against each other, as the enforcement of measurement threatens to eviscerate the aim of solidarity. Can the democratic capacity contract's promise be realized as long as measurement stalks its every instantiation?

· CHAPTER 2 ·

Manufacturing Anxiety

The Medicalization of Mental Defect

A T THE END OF THE EIGHTEENTH CENTURY IN FRANCE, Jean-Marc-Gaspard Itard undertook the first experiment to educate an idiot child, and he drew inspiration from John Locke. Locke may seem an unexpected muse for Itard; as chapter 1 documents, Locke believed idiots to be incapable of thought, speech, and action. Nevertheless, Itard set upon a six-year struggle to prove Locke's theory of education and, in so doing, inspired a new generation of physicians to take up the rehabilitation of idiots. By examining Itard and the medical practitioners after him, we see one reason why Locke's capacity contract is so seductive: by basing inclusion on cognitive capacity, Locke makes expansive democratic membership possible. Under this reading, excluded classes can demand membership on the erroneous charge of cognitive incompetence. For Itard and medical practitioners after him, their own burgeoning field could answer this possibility by crafting idiots into citizens. But these medical men needed more than a promise to gain public support; thus, they also sought to manufacture a deep anxiety about idiots' impulsivity, sexuality, and criminality as a central tactic to gain capital for their nascent field.

In this history, we see a face of anxiety that is less prominent in the field of disability studies. When discussing the roots of anxiety, activists and scholars often argue that the anxiety underwriting disability is primarily one of *contracting* disability. Confronting disability "triggers *in us* the recognition of our own vulnerability and porosity operating at the nucleus of our subjectivity."[1] Similarly, Paul Hunt—one of the most pivotal disability activists in the United Kingdom—argues that nondisabled people recoil from disabled people because the confrontation with disability provokes realizations of their own impending death.[2] Political theorists who take up issues of disability agree. Nancy Hirschmann argues that disability powerfully confounds the notion of the liberal sovereign self, explaining, "I could wake up tomorrow in intense pain, or be blinded or paralyzed in an accident."[3]

Thus, when we conceptualize ableist anxiety as one of contracting disability, challenges to ableism should aim to reconceptualize bodies from fixed to fluid. We see this challenge in disability rights activists' popular term TAB, "temporarily able-bodied." Disability and queer theorist Robert McRuer explains: "Sooner or later, if we live long enough (so we often say), we will all be-come disabled."[4] Similarly, Hirschmann writes, "The apprehension of disability forces individuals to come to grips with the way the body changes and can change further without warning, betraying the self's conception of who and what it is."[5] Together, these descriptions of apprehension suggest that if we alter how we see our bodies, then our fear of disability will dissipate.[6]

The fear of contracting disability is an important component of ableist anxiety, but there are problems with an ontological explanation of anxiety. First, as Bill Hughes explains, ontological claims that we are all vulnerable and thus all potentially disabled misses the political dimension of disability, particularly the experience of marginalization, exclusion, and stigma that accompanies disability and exceeds ontological claims.[7] For Hughes, "It may be 'good for the soul' to admit to ourselves that we are, or one day might become, the other that we (once) despised, but such moral clarity is unlikely to improve disabled people's standard of living or bring down the barriers that exclude them from participation in social and economic life."[8] Rather than further encode disability as the ontological sign of human limitation and decay, we could instead use disability to see the ways in which we are "bursting with possibilities and capabilities."[9] For Hughes, emphasizing the ways in which we are all vulnerable makes disability symbolize vulnerability rather than possibility.

But I also worry about the ways in which the apprehension of *becoming* disabled emphasizes the experience of *some* disabilities with the result of rendering other disabilities less visible. Authors refer to disabilities that result from accidents or age, but this emphasis largely sidesteps intellectual and developmental disabilities. Yet research finds that people harbor more negative attitudes toward people with intellectual and developmental disabilities than they do toward those with physical disabilities.[10] Why? Professionals classify intellectual and developmental disabilities in large part by their early onset, acquired at birth or during childhood. Thus, I cannot become intellectually or developmentally disabled.[11] So, although I might finish typing this sentence, get in my car, and have an accident that paralyzes me, I cannot wake up with Down syndrome. True, an accident might result in a traumatic brain injury, or if I live long enough, I might acquire dementia or Alzheimer's disease. But I cannot, by definition, enter into the class of people with intellectual and developmental disabilities. If I cannot wake up intellectually disabled, why am I so anxious about it?

I do not discount the fluidity of bodies, nor the anxiety over potential accidents or aging that may radically alter my level of capacity. My point is to move beyond ontological explanations of anxiety and instead look more closely at the historical and cultural production of ableist anxieties. More specifically, I recount the story about the ways in which medical professionals co-constructed intellectual disability and societal anxiety during the nineteenth and early part of the twentieth centuries. Medical professionals actively forged links between "idiocy" and anxiety as a way to garner public financial support and build legitimacy for their field. These anxieties gained momentum once medical professionals coupled idiocy with racial inferiority, thereby heightening the potential scale of civic degeneration.[12] This is an anxiety about living *with* the disabled. Thus, disavowing disability not only protects my psyche from an anxiety leveled at my own capacity but also aims to eradicate disability from the community.

Although the diagnosis of ableist anxiety as one of *becoming* disabled is compelling, it is incomplete. It simply misses the equally palpable anxiety of being *with* the disabled—an anxiety that we see historically manufactured. Additionally, a better understanding of racial and sexual oppression emerges when we couple our analysis of race, gender, and sexuality with the history of intellectual disability. To do so, I examine the "intersecting contracts" of Charles Mills and Carole Pateman, showing how attention to intellectual disability sharpens their analysis. The failure to take into account the history of people with intellectual and developmental disabilities leaves unproblematized the association between democratic membership and cognitive capacity. If left unproblematized, then the capacity contract has no internal mechanism to criticize the refusal of political standing to anyone who cannot pass a threshold level of rational capacity.

A Medical History of Idiocy

In the next three sections, I focus on three men—Jean-Marc-Gaspard Itard, John Langdon Down, and Henry Herbert Goddard—because of the pivotal role they played in defining intellectual disability and manufacturing anxiety. Each provides a glimpse into broader cultural trends of their time. In the first section, I describe the work of Jean-Marc-Gaspard Itard (1774–1838), whose experiment with Victor, a wild child discovered at the end of the eighteenth century, fused narratives of social contract theory, colonialism, and idiocy. Section two analyzes the ethnic classification of idiocy by John Langdon Down (1828–1896), whose categorization of Mongolian imbecility built on scientific studies of race. Section three explores eugenics through the figure of Henry Herbert Goddard (1866–1957), an American psychologist responsible for introducing the IQ test to the United States and creating an expansive categorization of mental defectiveness that fused racial degeneracy and feeblemindedness. Their treatments and analyses of idiocy demonstrate how they mobilized anxiety around the measurement of defective capacity and democratic communities.

Victor and Itard: A Broken Capacity Contract

In the French town of Aveyron in 1798, a group of hunters captured a mute eleven-year-old boy wandering naked and wild through the woods. Displayed in Paris to incite curiosity and revulsion, the boy joined a growing intrigue around feral children by European audiences.[13] The wild boy, named Victor by Itard, gave the young medical doctor an opportunity to test the sensationalist epistemology of John Locke, whom he credited with discovering the "most important truths," primary of which is that knowledge is gained entirely through experience.[14] Itard saw Victor as an alternative model for social contract theorists, whom he criticized for modeling the state of nature on barbarian society. "We ought," considered Itard, "to seek elsewhere the model of a man truly savage."[15] Like Locke, Itard staked inclusion on reasoning capacity, symbolized in language, and he saw Victor as an opportunity to build his own reputation by proving Locke's epistemology.

Pivotal to the intrigue around Victor was his uncertain status: was he an idiot or a boy truly savage? Dominant conceptions of idiocy at the time defined idiocy as a permanent state incapable of improvement. Philippe Pinel, the French physician who released the chains of inmates at Paris's Bicêtre and Salpêtrière asylums, thought the wild boy an idiot; as such, Pinel thought it useless to try to educate him. Itard, who was Pinel's student, disagreed and saw Victor not as "a hopeless idiot, but a being highly interesting."[16] Itard blamed Victor's lack of language on his abandonment from human community; as such, Victor was a true savage—not an idiot. Whether Victor was an idiot or a true savage would answer the question of whether he was teachable.

Similar to Locke's *Essay,* Victor's questionable capacity for rationality symbolized a divide between animal and human, and it was a divide on which Itard and his teacher, Pinel, disagreed. For Pinel, the boy's "whole existence [was] a life purely animal,"[17] and he was "inferior to some of our domestic animals."[18] Although Itard believed Victor educable, he emphasized the boy's instinctive habits. Victor was immune to sensations of extreme heat and cold: he could plunge his hand in fire or boiling water,[19] or roll half-naked in the snow.[20] His bodily movement was also interpreted as wild, often overtaken by "convulsive motions,"[21] leaping into the air, or squatting naked on the ground. The boy urinated on himself,[22] gnawed on his clothes and furniture,[23] and ate "disgustingly," "out of his hands besmeared with filth."[24] At times, Itard worried that Victor's accomplishments would be perceived as "only the common instinctive actions of an animal" or the "most common dog."[25]

Itard also interpreted Victor's behavior through the lens of savage society, even though Itard thought the boy entirely a product of wild isolation. "Like some savages in the warmer climates," Victor was "acquainted with four circumstances only; to sleep, to eat, to do nothing, and to run about in the fields."[26] For Victor, association with savage habits led to a unique kind of therapy. Convinced "that the inhabitants of the southern climates are indebted to the action of heat," Itard "thought it likewise necessary to put [Victor] in the hot bath for two or three hours every day, during which, water at the same temperature was frequently dashed on his head."[27] Itard described long hot baths as pleasurable for Victor—who consequently would not even get into a lukewarm tub—but not all of the physician's strategies were so benevolent.

Itard's interpretation of the boy as both savage and animal allowed him to inflict pain on Victor repeatedly through experimentation. He described stuffing Victor's nose painfully with snuff,[28] firing pistols near his ear,[29] exposing him naked to the cold,[30] repeatedly giving him electric shocks as the boy scrambled to get away,[31] and at one point suspending the boy face-first out a fourth-story window until the boy trembled in sweat and tears.[32] Itard seldom reflected on the ethical implications of these interventions. Itard considered mankind without intelligence to be inferior to many animals: "deprived of the characteristic faculties of his species, [he] drags on miserably, equally without intelligence and without affections, a life that is every moment subject to danger, and confined to the bare functions of animal nature."[33] Because the stakes of failure for Victor were so high—abandonment and dehumanization—any intervention seemed just.

The only stimulation that Itard disallowed was the use of tickling "when its effects were no longer confined to the production of pleasurable emotions; but appeared to extend themselves to the organs of generation, and to indicate some danger of awakening the sensations of premature puberty."[34] This passage is a rare glimpse into Victor as a sexual and gendered subject. Most accounts of wild children are male, but there were a few notable cases of wild girls captured as well. The fact that Victor could be stimulated sexually differed from other accounts of wild children, who seemed oblivious to the "other sex"—a trait that for some proved their idiocy.[35] Victor's precarious relationship to nonhuman animals may have rendered sexual stimulation too risky for Itard's experiment, as he needed to instill language into Victor rather than passion.

Itard's ability to hurt Victor coexisted smoothly with Itard's seeming devotion to the boy. Itard lovingly describes how each night Victor would open his arms for Itard's embrace, and then lie in bed as Itard tenderly stroked his face. In fact, it was this scene of affection—not the many stories of abuse—that Itard feared would prejudice his readers, who might perceive Itard's devotion as a loss of scientific credibility.

Itard thus paints an intimate picture of his life with Victor, and we seldom sense an anxiety on Itard's part that his own mental capacity would diminish, as if he could contract Victor's incompetence. Instead, the palpable anxiety for Itard is his own professional status: he desperately needed his experiment to work and for his readers to see Victor's improvements as proof of this success.

Despite Itard's promises and repeated experimentation over six years, however, Victor learned only a few words and never enough to engage in language—the true mark of reason. By 1806, long baths and vigorous exercise proved insufficient to curb Victor's enthusiasm for masturbation.[36] Itard abandoned his experiment and dedicated his career to educating deaf pupils. Overwhelmed by disappointment, Itard proclaimed, "Unfortunate! Since my pains are lost and my efforts fruitless, take yourself back to your forests and primitive tastes; or if your new wants make you dependent on society, suffer the penalty of being useless, and go to Bicêtre, there to die in wretchedness."[37] Itard's statement conjures both the wild savage with "primitive" tastes and the insane and idiotic inmates of Bicêtre. The inability to acquire language—as evidence of reason and human status—sealed Victor's abandonment.

Michael Newton characterizes Itard's relationship with Victor as a case of unrequited love. "It is not hard to feel as sorry for Itard as one feels for the wild child. For Victor's story catches hold of a vivid and tactful tenderness: its subject is ultimately that of yearning for and missing love."[38] Newton argues that this love was contaminated by the hardened and inescapable power differential between Itard and Victor. It may have been equally doomed by a cultural logic that dehumanized subjects who could not be rational: that for all Itard's assertions that Victor could have the same improvement as a dog and still be considered a success, it was simply insufficient. In contrast, David Mitchell and Sharon Snyder interpret Itard's story as "little more than a Western empiricist's fantasy."[39] But it can be equally read as the inevitable enforcement of the domination capacity contract: that human subjects incapable of cognitive competence are not human subjects after all.

Although Itard considered Victor a failure, his student Édouard Séguin (1812–1880) believed that Itard had experienced some success. Because Séguin considered Victor an idiot, the boy's minimal gains suggested that idiots were not entirely immune to instruction. Séguin immigrated to the United States, where he helped promote both a new taxonomy of idiocy and the growth of residential schools for the feebleminded in the mid-nineteenth century. Amid these promises of education, however, a residual category of uneducable idiots continued to stalk the parameters of human membership, instantiating the domination capacity contract.

Down's Measurements and the Mongoloid Idiot

When Seguin immigrated to the United States in 1850 (and Anglicized his name), he joined medical practitioners similarly convinced of the educability of idiots, including Samuel Gridley Howe, Hervey B. Wilbur, and William B. Fish. These men advocated for the construction of state institutions to educate idiots on the premise that rehabilitated idiots could rejoin their communities and be productive. By 1879, eleven institutions were functioning across the United States, with roughly fifteen hundred inmates.[40] Across the Atlantic, British medical doctor John Langdon Down was part of the growing field of medical practitioners advocating for the segregation of feebleminded children and adults. Down drew on theories of racial degeneration to better understand feeblemindedness, and he classified a new racialized type of Mongoloid idiocy.

Between 1858 and 1868, Down served as the superintendent of Earlswood Asylum for Idiots, the first institution for idiot children in Britain.[41] This period was significant for many reasons. Small private institutions for idiots began in Britain in the 1840s.[42] When Down stepped into Earlswood Asylum, the institution was growing, having consolidated the populations from two smaller institutions: Park House and Essex Hall. The growth of idiot asylums was in part an outgrowth of the overcrowding of almshouses, workhouses, and prisons, whose overseers considered idiots to be unsuitable occupants.[43] At the same time, Britain's construction of idiot asylums lagged behind that of the United States, and there was a push to catch up as a way to prove the country's level of modernization.[44]

Additionally, Down's tenure straddled a period in which the significance of idiocy was in flux. In the mid-nineteenth century, many professionals began to believe in the educability of idiots—the belief that idiots could be trained and returned to their communities. This "therapeutic optimism" underpinned the construction of idiot asylums.[45]

Down's tenure, however, also marked the encroaching pessimism over the educability of idiots, which would take hold by the end of the nineteenth century and link the growing population of idiots with racial degeneration and imperial decline.[46] The construction of institutions fed both outlooks—whether optimist or pessimist. Indeed, by 1875, two forms of institutions would exist: training schools for educable idiots and permanent residences for the rest.[47]

For Down, the consolidation of two asylums into Earlswood produced a "concentration of more 'idiots' under one roof than had ever occurred at any time or place in the world before."[48] This increased population enabled Down to classify residents on a scale never before undertaken. Drawing on the science of phrenology, Down measured and photographed all incoming residents, paying particular attention to idiots' skulls, mouths, ears, and palms.[49] Down's collection of photographs of residents remains the largest collection of clinical photographs from the Victorian era.[50] Down also conducted over two hundred autopsies at Earlswood, in which he measured the brains and organs of idiot children and adults.[51]

Like medical doctors in America and across Europe, Down used measurement and classification systems of idiocy to build his expertise and legitimacy. During his tenure at Earlswood, he published the article "Observations on an Ethnic Classification of Idiots," in which he described Caucasian, Ethiopian, Malay, and American Indian varieties of feeblemindedness.[52] He focused primarily, however, on the "numerous representatives" of the "great Mongolian family."[53] Down described them accordingly:

> The hair is not black, as in the real Mongol, but of a brownish colour, straight and scanty. The face is flat and broad, and destitute of prominence. . . . The tongue is long, thick, and is much roughened. The nose is small. The skin has a slight dirty yellowish tinge, and is deficient in elasticity, giving the appearance of being too large for the body.[54]

Down insisted that physical markers of idiocy could assist professionals in identifying and treating different categories of idiot children. By following the tenets of phrenology, which drew on racial, gendered, disabled, and animal identities, Down was part of a larger cultural trend that argued that the larger skulls of white upper-class men were indicative of mental and physiological superiority.[55] Down used his ethnic classification of idiots to defend monogenism—the belief that all races descended from the same human species—as opposed to polygenism—more popular in the United States—which stipulated that different races were also different species.

For Down, classifying idiots by ethnicity was valuable for medical professionals in part because it alleviated nurses and doctors from being charged with causing idiocy.[56] Classifying feeblemindedness by ethnicity also provided medical practitioners with specific guidance for educational intervention. For instance, Down believed Mongolian idiots were susceptible to heat, like their Mongol ethnic counterparts. By linking imbecility with ethnicity, Down carried over Itard's construction of idiocy. But unlike Itard—who used heat to stimulate Victor—Down believed the heat caused Mongolian imbeciles to regress. Echoing Itard's description of savage culture, Down argued that Mongolian imbeciles became more indolent during the spring and summer.

Down also fused constructions of race and idiocy to bolster the legitimacy of his growing profession. According to Down, only civilized nations concerned themselves with improving the conditions of idiots. "Probably nothing indicates more fully the onward progress of civilization than the thought that is now being given to the waifs and strays of humanity which are comprised in the subject of this paper. In a barbaric age the extermination of those who could not help the State, or tribe, was considered the wisest political economy."[57] Not only did savages help explain idiocy, but non-Western society was now depicted as too uncivilized to treat idiocy. Rather than promote egalitarianism, the educability of idiots reinforced relations of domination and subordination, both between medical professionals and the disabled, and between the West and non-West.

Classifying idiots into different categories also helped Down promote the large-scale segregation of idiots according "to their degree of intelligence, and capabilities of companionship." According to Down, "In small institutions there must necessarily be a commingling of the inmates and the consequent danger of disadvantage resulting from the influence of the least intelligent upon those who are higher in the scale."[58] By arguing for the importance of separating idiots by capacity within institutions, Down also promoted the separation of idiot children from their families. Down argued that idiot children of wealthy families were ignored, whereas for poor families, idiot children sapped the strength and sanity of mothers.[59] He admonished parents and other professionals who believed that idiot children could improve if surrounded by more intelligent peers. "Now, flattering as this may be to the parents, it is thoroughly baneful to the interests of the feeble-minded little one. . . . Intelligent children will not take part in the amusements and games of feeble-minded ones, moreover, there is no community of feeling or of interest."[60] Rather than promote growth, this commingling would only increase the idiot child's sense of isolation.

In this insistence on segregating idiots by level of capacity, we see how Down helped craft an anxiety of disability that arises *between* people due to incommensurate capacities. Down promised to ease this anxiety by first adding precision to the identification of idiots, then segregating them accordingly. Medical professionals thus played a crucial role in the alleviation of anxiety.

Indeed, Down often referenced the anxiety of parents—especially mothers—who worried about their child's slow development and, especially, lack of language. Down criticized other medical approaches that downplayed slow development as a way to try to ease the anxiety of parents. Instead, Down insisted that early diagnosis was essential. Part of parental anxiety stemmed from the unknown cause of idiocy. According to Down, parents feared that idiocy was hereditary and therefore due to their own degeneracy.[61] Thus, part of increasing the expertise of his field and alleviating parental anxiety was Down's fascination with tracing the cause of idiocy, whether accidental, genetic, or developmental.

Down believed that parental anxiety during pregnancy—especially for the mother—caused idiocy. According to Down, "in 32 per cent of my cases [there was] a well-founded history of great physical disturbance in the mother by frights, intense anxiety, or great emotional excitement."[62] This helped explain Down's findings that first-born children were more susceptible to idiocy due to the "exalted emotional life of the mother."[63] Here we see Down moving anxiety on to parents: anxiety that they caused the idiocy, parental anxiety itself as producing disability, and anxiety over determining idiocy. Down positioned himself and medical practitioners around him as capable of alleviating this anxiety:

they could diagnose idiocy, physically remove the idiot child from the family, and facilitate educational interventions in segregated settings.

The legacy of John Langdon Down is visible in the naming of Down syndrome, which replaced "mongol idiot" in the 1960s. Down's ethnic classification of feeblemindedness encountered problems when later researchers discovered that mongoloid children existed in African culture.[64] Because Africans were supposedly racially inferior to Mongoloid races, Mongoloid children for Africans would ostensibly be a sign of racial progress. Reginald Down, John Langdon's son, attempted to solve this problem by attributing the regression of mongolism to an earlier nonhuman origin of the human species. John Langdon Down had himself considered the close association between idiots and apes in correspondence with Charles Darwin. Both Langdon Down and Darwin saw apish characteristics in idiots, including the shape of their ears, brains, and excessive hairiness.[65] In *The Mongol in Our Midst,* W. G. Crookshank took up Reginald Down's theory and extended it, arguing that the three races of mankind—white, yellow, and black—mapped on to three distinct varieties of ape—chimpanzee, orangutan, and gorilla.[66] The compulsion to classify disability transgresses the border between human and animal as a way to instill community boundaries that help buttress theories of racial and increasingly gendered inferiority.

Goddard and Deborah: Anxiety Manufactured

Henry H. Goddard, an American psychologist and proponent of eugenics in the United States, built on nineteenth-century classifications of idiocy with race and gender to legitimize permanent institutionalization and sterilization. Unlike earlier practitioners who emphasized the idiot's educability to garner professional support, Goddard stressed the mental defective's hopelessness and sexual propagation as a way to heighten national anxiety. As institutions for the feebleminded swelled in size—a product of increasing immigrant labor, economic hardship, and an expansive definition of mental defectiveness—Goddard introduced a new objective: containment.[67] Anxiety over the uncontrollability of feeblemindedness necessitated a professional class that could identify and measure mental capacity and manage the containment of those falling short. This anxiety was not only about disability but about the American ideal of self-governance and whether disability could be sufficiently purged to enable this ideal to flourish.[68]

In 1912, Goddard published the best seller *The Kallikak Family: A Study in the Heredity of Feeble-Mindedness,* which connected the problem of idiocy to national anxiety.[69] Since 1906, Goddard had been director of research at the Training School for Feeble-Minded Girls and Boys in New Jersey. Family studies were popular in the late nineteenth and early twentieth centuries, the first of which was Richard Dugdale's *The Jukes: A Study in Crime, Pauperism, Disease and Heredity* in 1877. These histories were used to demonstrate the effects of heredity, despite their factually suspect content.[70] Goddard's *The Kallikak Family* supposedly proved the transmissible trait of feeblemindedness for the first time. Taking the surname by combining the Greek words *kallos* (good) and *kakos* (bad), Goddard traced the lineage of Deborah Kallikak, admitted to his institution for the feebleminded in 1910 at the age of eight.[71] Family studies had previously only traced the ancestry of degeneracy, but Goddard used Deborah's great-great-great grandfather Martin Kallikak to trace two lineages.

One of the primary ways that Goddard manufactured anxiety was to argue for the heritability of degeneracy. Deborah was the descendant of the first (*kakos*) lineage, which Goddard traced to her great-great-great grandfather's one-night drunken rendezvous with an idiot woman. The *kakos* lineage produced "143 feebleminded protégés, along with dozens of epileptics, alcoholics, prostitutes and common criminals."[72] Martin Kallikak later married a respectable Quaker woman, and their union together produced generations of good citizens, who married into the best families only, and thus produced the *kallos* line. In the *kallos* family, according to Goddard, "we find nothing but good representative citizenship. There are doctors, lawyers, judges, educators, traders, landholders, in short, respectable citizens, men and women prominent in every phase of social life."[73] Importantly, women played a central role in Goddard's story of degeneracy, as mating with the wrong woman had steep societal costs.

Not only was degeneracy heritable, but because Goddard tied mental defectiveness to sexual promiscuity, mental defects were fast outpopulating better stock. "There are Kallikak families all about us. They are multiplying at twice the rate of the general population, and not until we recognize this fact, and work on this basis, will we begin to solve

[our] social problem."[74] Goddard and eugenicists like him made mental degeneracy into a national anxiety.

One of the ways that Goddard was able to increase the population of feeblemindedness—and its concomitant anxiety—was by reclassifying feeblemindedness into three categories: idiot, imbecile, and moron. Idiots were the lowest grade, with "no higher intelligence than that of two-year-old children"; imbeciles had the equivalence in intelligence between three- and seven-year-olds; and morons—like Deborah—represented eight- to twelve-year-old arrested development.[75] Goddard was most concerned with the moron class because they were more likely to commit crimes, could influence lower-grade imbeciles into crime, and were the most difficult for the average person to identify.

Unlike nineteenth-century physicians who found physical markers of idiocy—weak chins, smaller sculls, overbites—Goddard emphasized the *absence* of physical differences to stir anxiety over morons. Goddard described Deborah as a "typical illustration of the mentality of a high-grade feeble-minded person, the moron, the delinquent, the kind of girl or woman that fills our reformatories."[76] Like many high-grade girls, Deborah was "good-looking, bright in appearance, with many attractive ways."[77] Hence, teachers failed to identify girls like Deborah as feebleminded, and this failure abetted feebleminded girls' downward spiral into moral degeneracy and prostitution. Goddard described Deborah's teachers as unwilling to see Deborah as feebleminded and thus mistakenly saw within her progress. Goddard used his criticism of teachers to assert his own expertise over feeblemindedness and the female teachers who worked with Deborah directly.

Because morons easily blended in with the nondefective, Goddard required a new scientific measurement for feeblemindedness—and an expert class of psychologists to administer the tests. In 1908, he introduced the Binet intelligence test to the United States. Not surprisingly, Goddard found exploding rates of feeblemindedness in the U.S. population. In 1917, Goddard tested the intelligence of World War I army recruits; 40 percent of white recruits were diagnosed feebleminded, while almost 90 percent of African American men were identified as mentally deficient.[78] On testing new arrivals to Ellis Island, Goddard found rates of feeblemindedness of 40 to 50 percent.[79] Hence, although white high-grade morons might pass as normal citizens, African Americans and many immigrants could be identified through their race or ethnicity.

Importantly, no amount of education could ameliorate the problem of feeblemindedness. Indeed, Deborah's "whole family was a living demonstration of the futility of trying to make desirable citizens from defective stock through making and enforcing compulsory education laws."[80] Careful to appease politicians and taxpayers, Goddard assured audiences that permanent incarceration would not inflate taxes.[81] Accordingly,

> if such colonies were provided in sufficient number to take care of all the distinctly feeble-minded cases in the community, they would very largely take the place of our present almshouses and prisons, and they would greatly decrease the number in our insane hospitals. Such colonies would save an annual loss in property and life, due to the action of these irresponsible people, sufficient to nearly, or quite, offset the expense of the new plant.[82]

Goddard's typology of feeblemindedness was crucial for the new custodial institution. Female high-grade morons could care for lower-grade imbeciles and idiots, while male morons could tend the farm.[83] Morons, according to Goddard, "are happy in doing their kind of work that you and I do not want to do. . . . In other words, we need these people. They are an essential element in the community."[84] Goddard's declaration that "we" needed morons also signaled a need for well-trained professionals, like himself, who could manage them. According to Goddard, "Not until we take care of this class and see to it that their lives are guided by intelligent people, shall we remove these sores from our social life."[85]

Goddard and other eugenicists manufactured an anxiety over the hopelessness of degeneracy, and we can see their success in legislative and judicial capacity contracts of their time: the Johnson-Lodge Immigration Act and the Supreme Court's decision in *Buck v. Bell*. The United States had already passed the Undesirables Act in 1882, denying the entry of idiots; but fueled in part by Goddard's results at Ellis Island, Congress passed the Johnson-Lodge Immigration Act in 1924 to limit drastically the numbers of nonwhite immigrants. The domination capacity contract thus functioned to deny entry to anyone who seemingly failed to pass a threshold level of rational capacity. Curbing immigration, however, could not eradicate the mentally defective population already reproducing in the United States.

Although half of all states "prohibited marriage between 'imbeciles, epileptics, paupers, drunkards, criminals, and the feebleminded'" in 1920,[86] Goddard and other prominent figures saw sterilization as an essential component of racial betterment. Institutional superintendents had used castration to curb the sexual behavior of low-grade idiots.[87] In fact, when first reported by the *Journal of the American Medical Association*, physicians considered vasectomies a useful tool for "chronic inebriates, imbeciles, perverts and paupers," along with "racial degeneracy."[88] In 1899, eight years before the legalization of sterilization in Indiana, Dr. Harry Sharp began performing vasectomies at the Indiana Reform School.

As states continued to legalize sterilization, it increasingly became a tool to use against feebleminded women.[89] According to Goddard, "one of the easiest things for [feebleminded girls] to fall into is a life of prostitution, because they have natural instincts with no power of control and no intelligence to understand the wiles and schemes of the white slaver, the cadet, or the individual seducer."[90] By describing feebleminded girls as victims to sexual predators, Goddard suggests that sterilization and permanent institutionalization is in the best interest of girls like Deborah.

Different forces pushed the bodies of feebleminded women to the forefront of state patrol. Licia Carlson argues that women "were particularly dangerous" to the nation because they were "the symbols of procreative power,"[91] but other forces contributed to this as well. Focusing on the period from 1870 to 1920, Louise Michele Newman argues that white women's sexuality was patrolled to protect the purity of the white race while also condoning white men's continued access to black, brown, and native bodies.[92] White suffragists also distinguished themselves from nonwhite and off-white women in order to stress their own moral superiority as a way to access political rights.[93]

Justice Oliver Wendell Holmes's decision in the Supreme Court case *Buck v. Bell* in 1927 is another form of the domination capacity contract, as individuals who fall below the threshold of rational capacity are denied the right to control their own sexuality. The state of Virginia fought to sterilize Carrie Buck, an unwed and poor seventeen-year-old girl, who represented the sexual promiscuity of poor, white mental defectives, despite the fact that she described her pregnancy as the result of sexual assault. Holmes's decision was rife with eugenic logic:

> We have seen more than once that the public welfare may call upon the best citizens for their lives. It would be strange if it could not call upon those who already sap the strength of the State for these lesser sacrifices, often not felt to be such by those concerned, to prevent our being swamped with incompetence. It is better for all the world, if instead of waiting to execute degenerate offspring for crime, or to let them starve for their imbecility, society can prevent those who are manifestly unfit from continuing their kind. The principle that sustains compulsory vaccination is broad enough to cover cutting the Fallopian tubes. . . . Three generations of imbeciles are enough.[94]

Carrie's sister, thirteen-year-old Doris, was also sterilized, but she did not realize it until much later in life. Doctors told her it was an appendectomy.

Buck's history illustrates the ways in which the identity of the intellectually disabled increasingly became a menace and a threat to an able-bodied, white, middle-class norm. This process was indebted to earlier histories, as described in the work of both John Langdon Down and Jean-Marc-Gaspard Itard. Goddard, more so than his predecessors, was able to fuse theories of racial degeneracy, sexual promiscuity, and mental defectiveness. In doing so, he promoted the containment, sterilization, and seclusion of people with disabilities as the surest way to curb anxieties over the health of the nation.

The Seduction of Compulsory Capacity

The twofold promises of Locke's capacity contract seduced Itard, Down, and Goddard: the promise that anyone who develops sufficient cognitive capacity can enter political and human communities, and the promise that the experts who can control the development of the less capable can have power over them. This is the seduction of compulsory capacity: when the "norm" of capacity is impossible to attain and yet is used to punish those who fall furthest from its attainment. Itard, Down, and Goddard followed the logic of compulsory capacity both in their attempts to rehabilitate idiots and in their campaign for permanent exclusion. The seduction of compulsory capacity travels well beyond these medical men, however, as we can find compulsory capacity in the history of American politics around disability and contemporary critical contract scholarship.

For example, in an analysis of political oppression in the United States, Douglas Baynton argues that political exclusion has been built on the accusation of disability, whereas inclusion is premised on revoking a disabled identity:

> Disability has functioned historically to justify inequality for disabled people themselves, but it has also done so for women and minority groups. That is, not only has it been considered justifiable to treat disabled people unequally, but the concept of disability has been used to justify discrimination against other groups by attributing disability to them.[95]

Baynton traces the entanglement of disability with race and sexuality in three pivotal debates in the Unites States: slavery, immigration, and the suffrage movement. Baynton also describes how suffragists deployed disability to defend their cause. For example, he describes a popular suffragist poster made in 1893 titled "American Woman and Her Political Peers." In the center is the portrait of Francis E. Willard, a prominent suffragette. Surrounding Willard are the faces of four similarly excluded figures: the convict, the idiot, the madman, and the American Indian. Henrietta Briggs-Wall, suffragette and designer of the poster, explained women's reactions: "It strikes the women every time. They do not realize that we are classed with idiots, criminals, and the insane as they do when they see that picture. Shocking? Well, it takes a shock to arouse some people to a sense of injustice and degradation."[96] The attribution of incapacity, for Briggs-Wall, constitutes an injustice. Claiming cognitive competence provides a legitimate claim to enter the political franchise and, as Baynton shows, seals the legitimate exclusion of people with intellectual disabilities.

Within the disability rights movement, the legacy of the capacity contract made it difficult for activists to resist appeals to compulsory capacity as a basis for inclusion and equality. We see compulsory capacity in foundational accounts of disability rights activism and scholarship. For instance, James Charlton's *Nothing about Us without Us: Disability Oppression and Empowerment*—a key text analyzing ableist oppression and the disability rights movement—builds on compulsory capacity to garner recognition for disabled people.[97] As Charlton explains the meaning of his title, overcoming oppression "requires people with disabilities to recognize their need to control and take responsibility for their own lives."[98] Charlton laments the absence of people with intellectual disabilities from his analysis, but he fails to see how his reliance on a Marxist understanding of oppression enforces exclusion. Under this logic, each individual must undergo a profound change in consciousness to understand his or her own oppression, but this assumes that an individual can conceptualize him- or herself as disabled. Likewise, Justin Dart, a disability activist, proclaims, "Empowerment is the issue of the age. . . . Nobody is going to give it to us. We have to empower ourselves."[99] R. R. Anspach similarly insists that the first step of a successful disability rights movement is to convince others by their actions that they are "independent, rational beings, capable of self-determination and political action."[100] Charlton, Dart, and Anspach endorse the logic of exclusion when they argue that full inclusion necessitates compliance with compulsory capacity—which poses real problems for the severely intellectually disabled.[101]

The seduction of compulsory capacity infiltrates disability studies scholarship as well, as scholars often hinge the empowerment of people with disabilities to the attainment of liberal models of agency. Cary Wolfe argues that disability studies scholars reclaim liberal models of agency at the expense of failing to trouble our overly cognitive understanding of agency. For Wolfe, "in its very attempt to recognize the unique difference and specific ethical value of the other, [the liberal humanist model] reinstates the very normative model of subjectivity that it insists is the problem in the first place."[102] Wolfe worries about the ways in which laws such as the Americans with Disabilities Act continue to center on a familiar liberal subject who conforms to the norms of compulsory capacity, such as "ability, activity, agency, and empowerment."[103]

Critical contract theory, pioneered by Carole Pateman's sexual contract and Charles Mills's racial contract, criticizes how demands for equality are imbricated in patterns of domination. Although my reading of the capacity contract follows in the critical contract tradition, we can see how Pateman and Mills fail to recognize the significance of disability. In particular, when Pateman and Mills explore the intersections of their sexual and racial contracts, they come very close to thinking about disability, but neither sees the ways in which sexual and racial oppression hinges on the exclusion of the intellectually disabled.[104]

In Mills's "Intersecting Contracts," he moves away from his dichotomy between personhood/subpersonhood that he developed in *The Racial Contract,* and instead suggests three categories of political standing: (1) person/contractor (white men), (2) subperson/subcontractor (black men and white women), and (3) nonperson/noncontractor (black women).[105] In this dynamic, black men and white women become partial signatories to the domination contract insofar as their political membership hinges on their willingness to endorse either sexism or racism. Black women, because they have neither whiteness nor masculinity to barter, have no political standing. Their exclusion is evident in the civil rights and feminist movements in the United States, both of which neglected the political needs of black women, as well as the pioneering work of black feminist scholarship, which calls attention to hybrid forms of marginalization. Mills neglects to add a fourth category to his contract: nonperson/noncontractor/subhuman. The medical history of people with intellectual disabilities often shows how they have constituted a fourth group of nonpersons—or even nonhumans.

Pateman's "Race, Sex, and Indifference" argues that the exclusion of nonwhites and women was legitimated by their supposed cognitive inferiority.[106] She fails to interrogate how the "lesser capacity for reason" is itself a kind of contract of domination that, rather than being just one component of the racial and sexual contracts, is also a system of oppression. Indeed, many of Pateman's examples of racial and sexual oppression similarly affected people with disabilities, but she never mentions their relevance. For instance, Pateman describes "fairs, ethnological exhibitions, and 'human zoos'" as public displays used to eroticize and marginalize nonwhite cultures.[107] Here, Pateman neglects the fact that disabled people were similarly treated as public spectacle. And though she discusses the consolidation of racist and sexist discourse in the advent of eugenics, she ignores the ways in which disability anchored and propelled eugenicist science and policies. Instead, Pateman construes "feeblemindedness" as just one of many traits that eugenicists used to oppress women and nonwhites, thus ignoring the thousands of disabled people institutionalized, sterilized, and euthanized.[108]

Just as political activists have colluded in the capacity contract, disability studies scholars argue that critical theorists are similarly prone to shirk any association with intellectual disability. Sharon Snyder and David Mitchell argue that queer, gender, and critical race discourses "have all participated to one degree or another in a philosophical lineage that seeks to distance those social categories from more 'real' biological incapacities."[109] Disavowing disability works to calcify disability as "true" insufficiency, and therefore legitimizes the basis for the political exclusion and mistreatment of people with disabilities.[110] Mitchell and Snyder, however, often collapse the distinction between physical and intellectual disabilities, particularly when they analyze the rationale and legacy of eugenics, thus erasing the ways in which the capacity contract is focused specifically on intellectual inferiority.[111] Indeed, although eugenicists targeted people with physical disabilities, they did so because of the ways in which physical defect signaled an inner intellectual or moral deficiency.

One of the reasons Mills and Pateman overlook the capacity contract is that while it bears resemblance to Mills's description of the domination contract, the goal of the capacity contract is different. Importantly, oppression can take many forms, with divergent purposes and opposing logics.[112] The racial, sexual, and capacity contracts have both overlapping and conflicting logics. The primary objective of the racial contract is to legitimize white exploitation of nonwhites, allowing whites to exploit nonwhites for both economic and sexual gain. The epistemological dimension of the racial contract obscures the logic of racism from whites, causing them to remain ignorant of their own role in the perpetuation of racism. The sexual contract, in contrast, "establishes men's political right over women [and the] orderly access by men to women's bodies."[113] In addition, the sexual contract enacts an epistemological divide, bifurcating the world into public and private spheres. Although the racial and sexual contracts subordinate both women and nonwhites, they nevertheless cast women and nonwhites as beneficial to their oppressors, due to their labor, sexual access, or both.

In contrast, the logic of the capacity contract is domination *and* disavowal. Unlike nonwhites, the intellectually disabled seldom represent an exploitable workforce, and more likely is the depiction of the disabled as economic drains on societal resources. This disavowal of the economic potential of disabled people actually works to hide the ways in which they are economically exploited. Indeed, just as Goddard used feebleminded inmates to propel institutions, people with disabilities continue to be employed legally in subminimum-wage positions in sheltered workshops and enclaves.

Intellectual disability similarly alters the meaning of sexuality, but seldom in terms of explicit exploitation. The sexuality of those with intellectual disabilities is primarily denied or prohibited, due to their depiction as asexual, sexually repulsive, or sexually irresponsible, particularly in relation to reproduction. In turn, this depiction renders invisible the sexual abuse of people with intellectual disabilities. Women and men with intellectual disabilities actually face increased risk for sexual assault. When people with intellectual disabilities do report sexual assault, authorities are less likely to believe them.[114] Thus, the capacity contract constructs disabled people as a class with little economic or sexual value, enacting an epistemology of disavowal in which the more able disavow their own chance of becoming disabled, their responsibilities to the disabled, and the actual lives of disabled people.

Despite these differences, there are similarities between the contracts. First, there are exploitation dimensions of the capacity contract. Like the sexual contract, the capacity contract removes disabled issues from public scrutiny, constraining the disabled to a permanent private existence. Additionally, the capacity contract's epistemology of disavowal shares many features with Pateman's settler contract. Pateman argues that the settler contract, in its strict form, "obliterates" the state of nature as a way to legitimize colonial conquest and the creation of white civil society, thus erasing nonwhite history.[115] But this erasure is incomplete. The state of nature haunts the white imagination, as it continually "acts as a threat and a warning of the disorder and nastiness that follow if the laws of the new state are not obeyed."[116] Disability has this same dynamic of the simultaneity of a disavowed but persistent presence.

By historically investigating the marginalization of disabled lives, we gain new theoretical insight into the ways in which oppression is both similar and different across intersecting identity groups. Moreover, because cognitive competence is a widely shared value—among activists, feminists, and critical theorists—we can begin to realize the difficulty of dismantling the capacity contract.

Conclusion: An Inescapable Contract?

If personhood is detached from requirements of rationality, on what grounds do the disempowered premise their political inclusion? What does empowerment look like without proclamations of self-competence as the basis for equality? Signatories to the capacity contract stipulate that only those capable of consent can achieve political equality. Whereas nonwhites and women can mount a charge of overcoming the wrongful ascription of irrationality, people with intellectual disabilities are constituted as a group by the shared feature of impaired mental functioning. True, *intellectual disability* is an umbrella term for all kinds of people with all degrees of impairment, from mild to severe. Many people with intellectual disabilities are capable of consent and reflection, and should thus count in the political franchise under the logic of the domination capacity contract. Embracing people with mild intellectual disabilities as political equals, however, only serves to reinscribe the capacity contract for the more profoundly disabled.

Undoing the capacity contract does not necessarily bode well for people with disabilities either. Once we remove cognitive competence as the principle marker of personhood and the political equality of disabled people is guaranteed, personhood suddenly loses political significance. The suggestion that people with profound intellectual disabilities *are* people seemingly empties the entire personhood category of relevance. The histories charted in this chapter document the porous boundary between people with intellectual disabilities and nonhuman animals, but we also see this porosity in contemporary philosophy. Peter Singer is, of course, emblematic of the belief that some nonhuman animals deserve more respect than do the intellectually disabled. His argument is all too familiar, but somehow philosophers and theorists never get tired of hearing it. Stefan Dolgert takes up intellectual disability and questions whether our conception of "neighbor" should expand to incorporate "walruses, porpoises, or spiders within its ambit."[117] You do not need to be a philosopher to know that comparison with bugs is not the political answer people with disabilities have been searching for. We see that our attention to people with intellectual disabilities and the question of their political status diverts us to the new focal point of nonhuman animals. For people with profound intellectual disabilities, social contract theory's rapture with rationality must be broken.

CHAPTER 3

The Disavowal of Disability
in Contemporary Contract Theory

PSYCHOLOGISTS FIND STARK INCONGRUITIES between our explicit and implicit beliefs about disability. "People are particularly unwilling to admit—or more likely, are unaware of—their implicit bias against individuals with disabilities."[1] Research confirms that most people harbor negative implicit attitudes about disability,[2] even as they believe that negative attitudes are socially unacceptable[3] and significantly impede the societal inclusion of people with disabilities.[4] The unconscious nature of ableist bias likely renders it more potent, as individuals fail to see their complicity with discriminatory behavior toward people with disabilities.

Likewise, the most pernicious philosophical biases against people with intellectual disabilities likely operate in our work implicitly. Feminist philosophers aiming to integrate people with intellectual disabilities within normative frameworks of justice primarily focus on the explicit exclusion of disability. Take, for example, feminist responses to John Rawls's removal of people with intellectual and severe disabilities from citizenship in *Political Liberalism*. Feminist philosophers intent on including all or most people with disabilities redefine key concepts—such as equality, trust, citizenship, or cooperation.[5] Rethinking these concepts is essential, but it may prove insufficient if the more general philosophical enterprise remains encrusted with implicit bias. Indeed, because many disability scholars and feminist theorists begin with Rawls's explicit disavowal of disability in *Political Liberalism,* they neglect how disability already saturates the foundation of his social contract theory.

Therefore, we need to look more closely at the ways in which underlying philosophical norms stigmatize people with intellectual disabilities. The first part of the chapter examines John Rawls's early philosophical work to exemplify both the explicit exclusion of disability and the more pernicious implicit traces of ableist prejudice. Rawls's work performs a *double disavowal* of disability: by claiming to set aside disability from full consideration, he disavows the epistemological function disability actually plays in his theory. In the second part of the chapter, I draw on the work of critical race, feminist, and disability studies scholars to show how they too marginalize people with intellectual disabilities. More specifically, diverse philosophical accounts ranging from liberal to feminist idealize the human capacity for knowledge as a keystone to democratic progress and thus cement negative meanings of intellectual disability.

John Rawls and the Disavowal of Disability

Rawls's work offers a fruitful starting place—not only because many philosophical accounts of disability use his work as a springboard but also because his theory has two foundational features that are well suited for promoting the full inclusion of all persons. First, Rawls insists that a theory of justice must accord "each member of society . . . an inviolability founded on justice which even the welfare of everyone else cannot override."[6] This fundamental commitment seemingly protects people with disabilities. Second, Rawls's construction of the original position as an imaginative device used to destabilize our thinking potentially offers a way to challenge ableist norms. These two foundational elements in Rawls's corpus—his substantive commitment to universal equality and his methodological tool to disrupt prejudice—seem *crafted* for a project on disability. What goes wrong?

Readers familiar with Rawls's work will recall that he "put[s] aside" people with mental disabilities in *Political Liberalism* because they are unable to cooperate in society and are inessential to the main questions of justice.[7] Rawls's language of *putting aside disability* and *waiting until the case can be examined* acts as if disability plays no part in his theory of justice.[8] In contrast, I argue that disability haunts Rawls's enterprise, as his early work draws on disability to define key conceptions and narrow his normative field. Rawls's reliance on ideal theory—in which he conceptualizes key themes without recourse to studying systematic patterns of injustice—obscures how disability functions throughout his work.

Like Locke's social contract, Rawls maintains the equality of each and every person, but his construction of personhood leaves him unable to recognize people with intellectual disabilities *as* people. Rawls's capacity contract thus *disables* the universal terms of his social contract. Substantively, the theories of Locke and Rawls share key features: both privilege rational capacity, depoliticize disability, and remove disability from the political sphere. The removal of disability, however, only occurs once disability's epistemological function—used to define personhood and politics—is exhausted. For both Locke and Rawls, intellectual disability divides personhood into normal and subnormal categories. But here the theorists' methods diverge. Although Rawls reinforces the *terms* of Locke's capacity contract, his method of ideal theory alters how the contract *functions* in social contract theory.

More specifically, because Locke's theory of knowledge requires consulting experience, he does not obscure idiocy's role. Rawls, in contrast, employs ideal theory, in which conceptions of the person and justice are seemingly formed without recourse to studying systematic patterns of injustice. The ideal dimension of Rawls's social contract theory forces him to enact a *double disavowal* of disability. By double disavowal, I refer to the ways in which Rawls's treatment of disability has two stages. At the first stage, Rawls draws on intellectual disability to define key conceptions, including personhood, the original position, and the principle of redress. This stage stigmatizes disability, marking disabled people as pitiful abnormalities and threats to limited national resources. Rawls's reliance on disability, however, is only one part of the problem. At the second stage, Rawls explicitly removes disability from theoretical consideration—for instance, removing disabled people from the scope of citizenship and health-care concerns. This explicit removal disavows the actual role disability already played. The two-stage aspect of disavowal—which first uses disability to define key conceptions and then disavows disability's prior theoretical role—is evident in Rawls's original position, his subcontract of advantage, and his discussion of redress. Significantly, we can think of each of these three instances as capacity contracts: each proscribes rules of fairness while normalizing threshold levels of compulsory capacity.

Compulsory capacity draws heavily on the work of disability studies scholars who link liberal promises of human perfectibility with the stigmatization of people with disabilities. For Robert McRuer, the "problem" of disability is the "inevitable impossibility, even as it is made compulsory, of an able-bodied identity."[9] Political philosophers since Aristotle have defined man by his cognitive capacities, but Rawls's location in the twentieth century positioned him at a point in time when ideal capacities collapsed into normal capacities—a move that naturalizes a fictional account of compulsory capacity. Lennard Davis argues that the twentieth century fostered a "new ideal of ranked order [that] is powered by the imperative of the norm, and then is supplemented by the notion of progress, human perfectibility, and the elimination of deviance, to create a dominating, hegemonic vision of what the human body should be."[10] David Mitchell and Sharon Snyder succinctly describe a "uniquely modern utopian fantasy of a future world uncontaminated by defective bodies."[11] Rawls's capacity contracts, which share in this modern utopian fantasy, evolved over the course of his career, many developing prior to the publication of his seminal work *A Theory of Justice* in 1971. Most of my interventions into Rawls's work begin not with his explicit exclusion of disability in *Political Liberalism* but with his work between 1951 and 1971, as he develops and then obscures his commitment to compulsory capacity.

Defining the Normal Range of Capacity

We can see Rawls's two stages of disavowal in his original position: he relies on disability to define moral agents' range of normal functioning while excluding issues surrounding disability from consideration. In the original position, agents are unaware of their exact intelligence, but they know their cognitive capacities fall within a "normal range."[12] Rawls specifies the normal range as follows: "Since the fundamental problem of justice concerns the relations among those who are full and active participants in society, . . . it is reasonable to assume that everyone has physical needs and psychological capacities within some normal range."[13] This explanation, however, fails to convey what constitutes the normal range; rather, Rawls assumes that he and his reader already know and share the same conception of what it means to be "full and active participants in society."

Although Rawls fails to specify the normal range, we can gain insight from an article he published in 1951, in which he draws on intelligence tests to define the normal range of moral reasoning. Rawls argues that moral insight demands "a certain requisite degree of intelligence, which may be thought of as that ability which intelligence tests are designed to measure."[14] By suggesting that we can discern "normal" functioning from intelligence tests, Rawls draws on the logic of statistical tests that fostered the creation and new idealization of normal. As Davis describes, American psychologists promoted IQ tests as a way to rank humans from the most intelligent (and superior in birth) to the mentally deficient. Intelligence tests transformed normal into a new ideal and created a subnormal category of existence—often symbolized by people with intellectual disabilities. As described in chapter 2, professionals like Henry H. Goddard used IQ tests to prove the inferiority of people with disabilities, African Americans, and immigrants.

For Davis, accompanying the ideal of a ranked order is the desire to eliminate deviance, and we see this in Rawls's removal of disability from the original position. According to Rawls, in reference to the "mentally defective," "besides prematurely introducing difficult questions that may take us beyond the theory of justice, the consideration of these hard cases can distract our moral perception by leading us to think of people distant from us whose fate arouses pity and anxiety."[15] Several troubling assumptions pervade this statement. First, Rawls suggests that moral agents' perception will function poorly if contaminated by anxiety and pity. It's not disability that Rawls is afraid his moral agents will contract but the anxiety surrounding it. Reason and anxiety thus oppose each other, and Rawls feels compelled to sanitize the original position—removing both disability and anxiety—to safeguard judgment.

Additionally, according to the dictates of ideal theory, moral agents in the original position are ignorant of the societal situation of people with intellectual disabilities in the nonideal world. Hence, they are unaware of societal prejudice, built barriers, failures in long-term care, and the spatial segregation of people with disability. Thus, the anxiety and pity that moral agents may experience if confronted with the mentally defective is entirely driven by the bare facts of disability—whatever those might be in a decontextualized world.

Finally, by describing the "mentally defective" as "distant from us," Rawls naturalizes human difference as insurmountable, as if disability is so abnormal as to be unimaginable, rather than a predictable aspect of human functioning across the life span. Rawls's description of "hard cases" as already "beyond" his theory of justice imports a false permanency of health and vitality into his description of "normal" functioning. Rawls adds, "the problem of justice concerns the relations among those who in the everyday course of things are full and active participants in society."[16] Like the language of normal and basic, Rawls's construction of "everyday course of things" assumes that confrontations with disabled people infrequently occur, if at all, and thus depoliticizes the twentieth century's forced segregation of people with disabilities.

By continually depicting moral agents in the original position as *normal* while emphasizing the *main* and *basic* questions of justice, Rawls constructs people with intellectual disabilities as peripheral to matters of justice and abnormal to human functioning. His oscillation between describing agents as ideal or normal intensifies compulsory capacity as both fictive and mandatory.

A Contract with the Least Able

Unlike the original position, which is designed to conceal differences in capacity, Rawls offers multiple iterations of a subcontract forged between the most and least advantaged—a subcontract moment in which individuals involved "do know their talents and abilities."[17] The contract of advantage first appears in the 1963 article "Constitutional Liberty and the Concept of Justice," then in the 1968 article "Distributive Justice: Some Addenda," then in 1971's *A Theory of Justice,* and finally in 2001's *Justice as Fairness: A Restatement.* Because Rawls repeatedly returns to this subcontract moment over a span of almost forty years, we can presume it is significant to his broader project. The evolution of this capacity contract discloses another instantiation of Rawls's double disavowal of disability, in which the terms of the initial contract proscribe different levels of capacity to moral agents. Over time, however, Rawls gradually obscures human capacity's role in the contract.

When Rawls first formulates the contract between the most and least advantaged, he fails to circumscribe agents' range of human capacities. In the contract of advantage of 1963, Rawls instructs us to "fix attention on two representative men, one for the upper and one for the lower ranges of ability."[18] Based on this description, people with dis-

abilities should occupy the least advantaged class. Indeed, Rawls conjures differences in ability when he describes the two men as the "more"
and "less able."[19] In this subcontract moment, each man must choose
between a caste society and a society ordered by Rawls's difference
principle.

The difference principle is part of one of the two principles of justice
that together form the main thrust of Rawls's theory. In the original position, moral agents could choose these two principles to guide the formation of politics and their society. The first principle, which is given
priority over the difference principle, gives all members of society the
same share of "basic liberty," including freedom of speech, religion, and
assembly. The second principle aims to ensure that social and economic inequalities are fair—that all people have an equal opportunity to
positions and offices—and, second, that all inequalities are to benefit
the least advantaged in society. This second component is the difference principle.

Consequently, economic inequalities are fair if they benefit the least
advantaged, and it is the subcontract of advantage that helps Rawls elu-
cidate the fairness of the difference principle. Moreover, it is the least
talented man who determines the subcontract's legitimacy, because the
most talented man will always choose the society ordered by the difference principle. With his reliable tool kit of talent and ability, the most
able man can assume that he will be successful in a society marked by
(some measure of) social and economic inequality. In contrast, the
caste society symbolizes for the most talented man the risk of subordination. If he is born into a lower class, his superior ability is
meaningless.

From the standpoint of the least able man, the choice appears quite
differently. Because he is on the "lower range of ability," he knows he
will be the least advantaged in Rawls's merit-informed economy. Although he will have the same share of basic rights and liberties as the
most able man, he will most likely have less money and less prestige. In
contrast, the caste society offers him the possibility of advantage: his potential birth into the upper class can secure what his lackluster abilities
cannot. Rawls argues, however, that the less able man is better off in the
society of the two principles of justice because any advantages that ac-
crue to the most advantaged must also improve the lives of the least
talented. We assume quite the opposite in the caste society: the most

advantaged have no incentive to improve the lives of the less fortunate. Thus, the least able man will avoid risking the slim possibility of social and economic privilege and will instead opt for the guarantee of equal liberty and the resignation to economic and social inequality.

Rawls's subcontract discloses disturbing assumptions about the naturalization of inequality, but it also offers us a way to judge the distribution of privilege. On the one hand, we see in Rawls's "original" subcontract certain disabling assumptions already at work, most important of which is that the least advantaged class perfectly maps onto the least able. Rawls fixes disabled and abled categories to different socioeconomic conditions, and he naturalizes the "worse off" as an obvious outcome of impairment. On the other hand, because the subcontract ensures that any benefit to the most advantaged will equally improve the lives of those on the "lower range of ability," it potentially raises important questions about societal relationships between the disabled and the abled. For instance, how do we design a world in which every advantage of the abled similarly enhances the lives of the disabled?

But Rawls forestalls any radical reenvisioning of abled-disabled relations as he gradually idealizes the class of "least advantaged." In "Distributive Justice: Some Addenda" (1968), Rawls contends "the least advantaged are represented by the typical unskilled worker."[20] By 1971, with the publication of *A Theory of Justice*, Rawls circumscribes the least advantaged to either the "unskilled worker" or those whose income is comparable to the least skilled.[21] Rawls acknowledges that these inequalities may be the result of "natural characteristics," such as sex, race, or culture, and moreover, that this kind of inequality is "seldom, if ever, to the advantage of the less favored."[22] But he no longer mentions capacity. Indeed, Rawls eliminates any descriptions of the least advantaged as the "less able" on "the lower ranges of ability." He seems to have intentionally but quietly displaced the role of capacity as a characteristic of a dis/advantage that is morally arbitrary. Yet the earlier subcontract haunts the newer instantiation, shadowing the unskilled worker with the assumption that he is an unskilled worker *because* of his lesser capacity.

By removing differences in capacity, Rawls also alters the terms of the agreement for the most talented. Because the most able man assumes that he will be the most economically privileged, *whom* he contracts with is significant. According to the difference principle, he must consent to redistributing some of his wealth to maintain fairness. The terms of redistribution will change according to the range of capacities present. For example, Amartya Sen shows that people with disabilities may need a larger share of resources to convert into the same level of capabilities as nondisabled citizens. In other words, the cost of freedom of mobility and equal participation will be higher for some people with disabilities.[23] Thus, the redistribution of wealth will be more significant. By removing radical differences in capacity from the subcontract, the most able man cannot comprehend the consequences of his agreement to economic and social inequalities. Disability is thus out of sight, out of mind, and outside politics.

In the development of Rawls's subcontract, the double disavowal of disability is clear: we see him define disadvantage in relation to capacity, but then remove the least able from political consideration. Rawls's subcontract is potentially a tool to think about disability: to better understand the ways in which societal structures generate disadvantage. However, Rawls's subcontract's evolution renders differences in capacity politically irrelevant. We also see why setting aside disability is so troublesome: because individuals consent to distribute advantage only among those who possess a threshold level of capacity, widening the range of capacity drastically alters the terms of agreement. By circumscribing the range of human capacities, Rawls constructs an artificial society in which differences in capacities are meaningful and yet minimized.

Redress and the Defective

Like the original position and the contract of advantage, Rawls's discussion of redress—first in 1968 and then again in 1971—potentially offers a radical way to envision the demands of equality for people with intellectual disabilities. Indeed, Rawls uses differences in human capacity to explain and legitimize redress, as any society intent on ensuring equality should be concerned about how inequalities of capacity threaten to map onto political inequalities. Careful examination, however, suggests no such radicalization. Instead, only individuals with a narrow range of human capacities fall under the purview of redress for Rawls, thereby depoliticizing societal responsibilities toward people with disabilities.

For Rawls, redress requires political interventions to remedy human inequalities, and he argues that redress is essential to any theory of justice. Intellectual disability seemingly qualifies for considerations of redress, "since inequalities of birth and natural endowment are undeserved," and "these inequalities are to be somehow compensated for." Rawls continues,

> In order to treat all persons equally, society must give more attention to those with fewer native assets and to those born into the less favorable social positions. . . . In pursuit of this principle greater resources might be spent on the education of the less rather than the more intelligent, at least over a certain time of life, say the earlier years of school.[24]

Rawls continues, arguing that levels of intelligence are "simply natural facts. What is just and unjust is the way that institutions deal with these facts."[25] Rawls's descriptions suggest both limitations and possibilities for a disability politic.

On the one hand, there are problems with the ways in which Rawls refers to "fewer native assets" and differences in capacity as "simply natural facts." Both descriptions conform to a medical model that understands disability as something arising naturally out of the body rather than as a cultural phenomenon created through patterns of inequality and discrimination that stigmatize some bodies over others. As earlier described by disability studies scholar Davis, norms of intelligence and the means of measuring intelligence are highly contested. Indeed, what are "native assets"? Rawls seems to suggest that we can easily tease apart both biological abilities and the social realities that produce those abilities.[26]

On the other hand, by focusing on the ways in which "institutions deal with these facts," Rawls shifts the significance of differences in capacity to societal relationships. Thus, how we design institutions and respond to human differences in ability comprise the basic problem of justice. Although Rawls clearly follows a medical model of disability, his focus on institutions invites a kind of social model interpretation of disability, which brackets off bodily or mental impairment and focuses on the ways in which institutions and systematic prejudice create and respond to disability.

I suggest that we can piece together more of Rawls's outlook on disability by analyzing his footnotes in the section on redress. When Rawls states that "undeserved inequalities call for redress," he chooses for evidence two articles in which authors use people with disabilities to modify the obligations associated with redress. Because Rawls seldom cites work in footnotes and because these citations recur as he refines his argument over redress, we can infer that Rawls accords these references considerable importance. These include a 1950 article, "Justice and Liberty," by D. D. Raphael and a 1944 article, "A Defense of Human Equality," by Herbert Spiegelberg.[27] Raphael and Spiegelberg disagree regarding the treatment of disabled people: Raphael accords them unequal treatment to ensure their well-being, whereas Spiegelberg worries that redressing handicaps threatens to dull the talents of the most privileged. These authors help us more fully piece together a picture of disability: both authors sharply divide the defective from the normal and presume an overriding assumption about the misery of disabled lives.

Rawls cites Raphael in his 1968 and 1971 discussions of redress, immediately after stating that "undeserved inequalities call for redress."[28] According to Raphael,

we think it right to make special provision for those affected by special needs, through natural disability, such as mental or physical weakness.... We attempt to remedy, so far as we can, the inequality of nature.... The inequality of treatment is an attempt to reduce the existing inequality, to bring the needy person up to the same level of advantages as the normal.[29]

Repeatedly, Raphael distinguishes between the "needy" and the "normal." While "we" (the nondisabled/normal) cannot make "them" (the disabled/needy) equal, Raphael argues that we are obligated to care for them.[30] Raphael depicts the disabled as pitiful people whose lives are never worthwhile. Accordingly, "our recognition of 'special' needs is a recognition that some persons, by reasons of nature or accident, fall below the normal level of satisfactions, below the level which most people enjoy and which we regard as essential for decent living."[31] Raphael's take on disability seems aligned with Rawls's depiction of the mentally defective as arousing pity for moral agents. Although Raphael stigmatizes disability, he also uses it to expand the reach of redress.

In contrast, Spiegelberg uses disability to limit redress, and importantly, Rawls agrees: "We are to weigh [redress] against the principle to improve the average standard of life, or to advance the common good."[32] Rawls states this passage twice—first in 1968 and again in 1971—and both times, he adds a footnote to Spiegelberg. In the passages cited, Spiegelberg addresses the risks posed by redress, especially when redress disadvantages the most privileged. For Spiegelberg, "it should be considered that the destruction of native advantages may easily constitute a cruel injustice against the better equipped individual."[33] Disability helps Spiegelberg explain this form of cruel injustice: "In the case of the mentally handicapped this would amount to inflicting upon him an extra dose of training, obviously with a very dubious chance of success and in all probability even against his definite desire."[34] For Spiegelberg, improving the lives of people with disabilities threatens the common good, as it wastes an inordinate amount of resources to enhance the well-being of disabled people—a goal with minimal success at best. Rawls seems to agree, arguing that the difference principle "does not require society to try to even out handicaps as if all were expected to compete on a fair basis in the same race."[35] Rawls fails to clarify which handicaps are under societal domain and which are provinces of nature. Rawls's capacity contracts, which narrow the range of human abilities under political consideration, seem to depoliticize human incapacity in proportion to the impairment's severity. If Raphael helps us understand Rawls's assumption that disability arouses pity, then Spiegelberg suggests why Rawls might have considered disability to induce anxiety, as disabled people threaten to drain scarce resources and stifle the development of the most talented.

In concluding his section on redress, Rawls states that he "shall not consider questions of eugenics," and yet familiarity with the logic of eugenics suggests that Rawls did not escape from eugenic thinking. Indeed, even in his construction of natural assets, Rawls is drawing on prior eugenic thinking, particularly that of Sir Francis Galton, one of the most pivotal eugenic thinkers. It was Galton who coined the phrase "nature versus nurture," and he believed in the realities of "native assets" as biologically given and immutable. But eugenic thinking is pronounced in Rawls as well.[36]

Immediately after he suggests that he will not consider eugenics, Rawls ties the promise of liberal equality to the improvement of human capacities. According to Rawls, "over time a society is to take steps at least to preserve the general level of natural abilities and to prevent the diffusion of serious defects."[37] Consequently, "it is possible to adopt eugenic policies, more or less explicit" because it is "in the interest of each to have greater natural assets."[38] Rawls fails to consider the ways in which his own theory of justice privileges some people, first by treating their abilities as biologically given and then by limiting their responsibility to people with impairments. Rawls continues: "We might conjecture that in the long run, if there is an upper bound on ability, we would eventually reach a society with the greatest equal liberty the members of which enjoy the greatest equal talent."[39] Rawls clearly equates greater capacity with greater liberty, thereby marking disability as an essential threat to liberal progress.

Using the work of Spiegelberg and Raphael to reconstruct the image of the mentally defective reveals another instance of double disavowal in Rawls's discussion of redress. Again, we see Rawls conjure differences in human capacity to help legitimize redress, but then exclude some forms of human difference from political consideration. The work of Spiegelberg and Raphael also helps us understand the potent and widespread anxiety that threatens Rawls's moral agents in the original position. It is not an anxiety of whether or not agents have or will acquire a disability; indeed, Rawls has already assuaged moral agents of this fear, as they know their capacities fall within a "normal" range. It is instead a more pervasive anxiety that threatens moral agents: the anxiety of existing in a world *with* the disabled. For each theorist, disability is an abnormal failure of human functioning that erodes the well-being of liberal society.

Feminist and Critical Capacity Contracts

In this section, I analyze the ways in which critical and feminist theorists critique Rawls's commitment to compulsory capacity, but then revert to an idealized cognitive subject to anchor democratic progress. These critical capacity contracts continue to disavow disability, either by failing to comprehend fully the function of disability in Rawls's work or by relying on citizens' cognitive capacities to remedy the consequences of deeply embedded theoretical exclusions. My purpose is not to mark these theorists as hypocritical but to show their deeply troubled and yet sticky commitment to compulsory capacity.

Adding Disability into the Contract

One of the problems with works that take up issues of disability in Rawls is that they assume that Rawls is excluding disability and thereby overlook the ways in which disability already saturates Rawls's theory of justice. We see this in Martha Nussbaum's treatment of Rawls, as she assumes that social contract theorists have simply omitted disability from their theories. "These problems," as she describes them in relation to disability, "cannot be ignored or postponed on the grounds that they affect only a small number of people."[40] Her depiction of the problem in Rawls as a mere postponement fails to grasp the depths to which disability already pervades his normative framework of justice. This move only concedes the second stage of disavowal and thus misses the important defining work that occurs at the first stage.

As Nussbaum's discussion suggests, this kind of approach assumes that disability is absent from social contract theory more broadly. Christie Hartley and Licia Carlson and Eva Feder Kittay refer to the absence of people with intellectual disabilities from political thought.[41] While I agree that people with intellectual disabilities appear only recently in political theory as an oppressed category, it is erroneous to assume that they simply never appear in the canon of political theory. Chapter 1 detailed how disability circulates across Locke's corpus, helping him draw the boundaries of human understanding. Critical disability scholars argue that disabled people surface often as narrative tropes, used to symbolize death, foreboding, or malevolent natures in literature.[42] Likewise, I expect that if we investigate the history of political thought more broadly, we will find disability performing important theoretical work.[43]

Lowering the Capacity Threshold

Recent feminist work—by Sophia Wong, Christie Hartley, and Anita Silvers and Leslie Pickering Francis—aims to restore the promise of Rawls's egalitarianism by working within a contractual framework to include all or most people with disabilities.[44] These interventions aim to correct Rawls's exclusion, but many share Rawls's resignation that justice cannot encompass people with the most severe disabilities. As such, these feminist capacity contracts fail to dislodge Rawls's ranked order of capacities and thus fail to wrestle fully with underlying ableist prejudice.

Wong argues that we should understand Rawls's two moral powers of citizenship as potential capacities that require certain enabling conditions, such as education, relationships, and human interaction. Because we cannot identify which human beings will develop these capacities, we need to ensure the full set of enabling conditions for all individuals. Wong uses as evidence people with intellectual disabilities who were abandoned in institutions but later gained important cognitive skills, making them capable of Rawls's moral powers. While Wong offers essential insight into the history of people with intellectual disabilities, I worry that her approach concedes too much to Rawls's conception of citizens. By retaining the two moral powers of citizenship, Wong neglects how persons with profound intellectual impairments may be able to contribute to society even if they lack the requisite abilities. Moreover, returning to Davis's idea of a ranked order, Wong's maintenance of Rawls's moral powers leaves intact ableist norms that rank individuals by their capacities.

Hartley reinterprets Rawls's social contract theory to include most people with intellectual disabilities, arguing that those "who can make a cooperative contribution to a society based on mutual respect should be viewed as members of society entitled to justice."[45] Most people with intellectual disabilities—even if they lack Rawls's two moral powers—participate in the labor market, "engage in mutually supportive relationships," and help others develop important human values, such as humility and kindness.[46] Hartley thus offers a capacity contract with minimal capacities required. Hartley's cooperation, however, hinges on nondisabled people's willingness to engage with the disabled—to form mutually supportive relationships with them or to learn important lessons of kindness from them. Psychological research into ableist attitudes, however, unsettles this assumption. Faced with ableist prejudice, people with severe intellectual disabilities may find few people willing to engage with them who can thus prove their cooperative potential.[47] In addition, Hartley admits that some people with severe disabilities will be unable to cooperate, but like Rawls, she suggests that principles outside justice will preside over these rare cases.[48]

Accordingly, the approaches of Hartley and Wong may be insufficient to undermine the exclusionary force of Rawls's capacity contracts, a point they share with Nussbaum's capabilities approach. While attempting to dismantle ableist assumptions within social contract theory, Nussbaum concludes that the condition of "a permanent *vegetative* state of a (former) human being . . . is not a human life at all, in any meaningful way."[49] In her insistence that "the social goal should be understood in terms of getting citizens above this capability threshold," Nussbaum enforces compulsory capacity as the foundation of her approach.

Silvers and Francis's revision of social contract theory to be "more like a project for engendering trust than a bargaining session" seems the most promising intervention.[50] They argue that most people with intellectual disabilities can give or withhold trust. For those who cannot, their societal presence can bolster trust for all participants, "for people's trust in whether a society really understands and is committed to justice is influenced by whether inferior treatment of the disabled and other 'outliers' is prohibited or permitted."[51] While Silvers and Francis effectively dislodge individual capacity as a requirement of social contract theory, they seem to presume that nondisabled people possess a high level of concern for the quality of treatment shown to people with severe disabilities — an assumption again weakened by entrenched ableist prejudice.

Each of these approaches foregrounds the capacities of citizens as the starting point for political evaluation. Moreover, they provide us with a narrow set of theoretical options within social contract theory. Hartley's typology between contractualism and contractarianism, for instance, neglects a third option of critical contract theory propelled especially by Charles Mills, which seems best equipped to unravel the domination of compulsory capacity.

Developing Capacities—and Disavowal

Charles Mills's treatment of race and social contract theory offers fruitful inroads for a project on disability, as Mills specifically targets Rawls's depoliticized construction of rational capacity. For Mills, Rawls's reliance on ideal theory sustains the "systematic omission" and "evasion" of racial oppression.[52] Mills focuses on the ways in which ideal theory specifically idealizes cognitive capacities:

> The human agents as visualized in the theory will also often have completely unrealistic capacities attributed to them—unrealistic even for the privileged minority, let alone those subordinated in different ways, who would not have had an equal opportunity for their natural capacities to develop, and who would in fact typically be disabled in crucial respects.[53]

Ideal theory promotes two distinct fictions in relation to idealized capacities: it neglects inequalities in cognitive capacities—whether these inequalities are caused by injustice or impairment—and it exaggerates the abilities of the privileged, constituting a class of not just able-bodied but super-bodied agents. Disabled capacities, however, are an outcome of systematic injustice for Mills, and he avoids the ways in which Rawls excludes people with disabilities.

Mills argues that racism causes an epistemology of ignorance, in which "cognitive dysfunctions" leave whites "unable to understand" because they live in a "cognitive model that precludes self-transparency."[54] Mills describes the racial contract as promoting an epistemology of ignorance among (most) whites, in which white people are ignorant of their own complicity with racism. In many ways, we can import Mills's description of the effects of the racial contract onto Rawls's treatment of disability. For example, for Mills, the "cultivation of patterns of affect and empathy . . . are only weakly, if at all, influenced by nonwhite [disabled] suffering."[55] Moreover, in the racial contract, "evasion and self-deception thus become the epistemic norm,"[56] as certain nonwhite/disabled "realities [are] made invisible."[57]

If the problem is ignorance for Mills, then the answer is to become more cognizant, both for whites and nonwhites. If whites live in a "racial fairyland," nonwhites must launch a cognitive voyage to overturn racism.[58] "One has to learn to trust one's own cognitive powers, to develop one's own concepts, insights, modes of explanation, overarching theories, and to oppose the epistemic hegemony of conceptual frameworks designed in part to thwart and suppress the exploration of such matters; one has to think *against the grain*."[59] Similarly, Licia Carlson refers to an epistemology of ignorance among philosophers around disability, suggesting that if we knew more about people with disabilities and their histories, we could craft better theories.[60]

Mills is not the first to propose cognitive self-consciousness raising as a first step to emancipatory politics, but judged from the lens of intellectual disability, this familiar route to empowerment is troublesome. Mills thus straddles a strange divide: he critiques Rawls's construction of ideal cognitive capacities as a source of inequality but then calls on the production of heightened cognitive skills to combat inequality.

While an epistemology of ignorance captures many components of domination, the language of ignorance seems ill-advised for an emancipatory project around intellectual disability, namely because of the ways in which the familiar Enlightenment category of ignorant/cognizant maps onto morally wrong/right. For Mills, ignorance shrouds the morally inferior, whereas the cognitively superior are also morally superior. Better politics demands smarter people.

Another critical approach to Rawls is offered by Iris Young, who integrates queer theory to demonstrate how Rawls's conception of personhood normalizes one particular kind of identity by rendering deviant alternative ways of being in the world. For Young, the "situation of people with disabilities illustrates the problems of normalization most starkly."[61] She criticizes philosophers' assumption "that lacking specific bodily or mental functionings automatically makes a person less competent than those that have them."[62] Offering the example of a person in a wheelchair, Young argues that readdressing architectural barriers alters the contribution potential of disabled populations to the public. With inclusive attitudes and accessible spaces, disability disappears.

Although essential, Young's critique is incomplete. She recognizes how normalization affects people with disabilities, but her own example of wheelchair users threatens to reinforce the precariousness of people with intellectual disabilities. With physical obstacles removed, the wheelchair user can now achieve Rawls's construction of human behavior in the "usual sense" by contributing to society. Although Young is drawing our attention to the ways in which society creates disability, she is also reaffirming that the *usual* way of being in the world is productive and capable, thereby sustaining the stigma against people with profound disabilities.

Another reason to discard the language of ignorance is the different kinds of oppression at work behind ableism and racism. Ignorance promotes invisibility. As Mills's critique of Rawls reveals, issues of race seldom surface.[63] White privilege sustains philosophers' evasion of race.[64] In contrast, disavowal exceeds disappearance. Young understands this in her description of the paradoxical quality of normalization: deviant groups are both invisible *and* hypervisible. We see this in the political thought of Rawls, in which, unlike race, the threat of disability circulates *all the time*. Disability is present and yet forgotten, palpable and yet invisible, recurring but aberrant. Psychological insight into the multilayered account of bias helps us understand disability's complex position in philosophy: whether we explicitly aim to exclude or include it, implicit negative assumptions about disability persist.

These critical and feminist approaches thus reveal how we continue to disavow the severity of some disabilities, as if convincing ourselves that by engineering societal structures and increasing knowledge we can eradicate intellectual disabilities entirely. In these multiple ways, critical interventions into mainstream philosophy's treatment of disability heighten the ideal of compulsory capacity and minimize cognitive difference as soon as it glimpses its possibility.

In making claims about ignorance and knowledge, critics of Rawls have more in common with his epistemology than they suspect. Both the original position and an epistemology of ignorance offer us intellectual agendas that promise knowable political transformations. Whether we are to choose political principles from behind the veil of ignorance or launch onto a course of rigorous education to overturn prejudice, these directions encase intellectuals in a purposeful and righteous agenda. In this we glimpse again that always confident, cognitively ideal self: she grasps the problem; she knows the solution. If political transformation fails to occur as her epistemology promised, then the fault falls on the ignorant, who are unaware of and uncommitted to an emancipatory politic. In contrast, an epistemology of disavowal upsets our cognitively ideal fantasyland. Even if we increase our knowledge about disability, our biases may continue operating implicitly. Indeed, people with more education and higher incomes are more likely to prefer death to disability.[65] In a profession defined by cognitive demands, academics may harbor deep anxieties about cognitive incapacity that likely seep into our theoretical norms.

Conclusion: An Epistemology of Disavowal

Why focus so much attention on anxiety amid all the political obstacles facing people with disabilities, such as poverty, unemployment, abuse, and the criminal justice system? Unraveling anxiety is a key component of advancing disability rights, and yet scholars seldom discuss strategies we can employ to do so. Instead, scholars often give us the example of advancing disability rights through the example of the wheelchair user. Using the social model of disability, scholars argue that providing more ramps increases the accessibility for all people and radically upends what it means to be able-bodied and disabled.[66] While I agree, I believe there are limitations to this example. First, changing the environment so that the wheelchair user has more accessibility avoids the interpersonal component of ableism in that it promotes everyone's accessibility and requires very little behavioral modifications of the abled. Indeed, the abled need not sacrifice any of their own privilege in their support of ramps. But confronting the problem of anxiety forces us to rethink the ways in which we engage (or fail to engage) across radical differences in cognitive capacities. Promoting inclusion may not be so easy—it may in fact be discombobulating, as dominant norms of interaction are likely to be upended, ignored, and challenged.

Indeed, when Rawls's *A Theory of Justice* was first published in 1971, it was still legal for states to prohibit children with disabilities from attending public schools—and it was justified, in part, on the premise that teachers and nondisabled students would be too nauseated from the presence of students with disabilities.[67] Like Rawls's discussion of redress, legal experts presumed that disabled students would not benefit by education and, moreover, that their presence would interfere with the education of the more abled.[68]

Just as ignorance is the flip side of knowledge, countering disavowal requires confronting our anxiety. Researchers repeatedly find that contact with disabled people is the most reliable predictor of positive attitudes toward people with intellectual disabilities.[69] Contact is effective, I believe, because it makes disavowal untenable, as it reveals to us our own implicit bias, making it difficult if not impossible to continue disavowing our negative attitudes. Interpersonal contact also requires us to rethink our modes of interaction, asking how cognitive privilege enforces norms that penalize and exclude others. Insofar as our philosophical work captures this democratic mode of contact, we may better accomplish inclusion. Both Eva Feder Kittay and Sophia Isako Wong offer us examples of philosophically engineered contact, enfolding their philosophies in narratives, histories, and photographs of people with intellectual disabilities.[70] Chapter 4 pursues this method of textual contact, as it integrates my observations of self-advocates with intellectual and developmental disabilities.

Additionally, feminist philosophers like Kittay and Carlson upend the philosophical project from one of knowing to one of *unknowing*. For example, Kittay issues two new rules for philosophers: epistemic responsibility and epistemic modesty.[71] First, if philosophers are going to consider the issue of disability, then they are responsible for knowing the actual lives of disabled people. If they refuse to do so, then they must acknowledge their own epistemic modesty or, as Kittay says, "know what you don't know."[72] Kittay inverts philosophers' relationship to intellectual disability by emphasizing philosophers' limited cognitive capacities. Similarly, Carlson suggests that "the complexity of intellectual disability as a lived experience suggests that some barriers to knowledge for those who are not defined as intellectually disabled may be insurmountable, either temporarily or perhaps permanently."[73] Here, Carlson and Kittay argue that acknowledging the *limits* of knowledge is necessary for expanding justice for people with disabilities.

Perhaps this is why philosophy poses so much resistance to inclusive projects for people with intellectual disabilities: because the physical spaces we inhabit to pursue philosophical thought discriminate on the basis of cognitive capacity and because our philosophical solutions to democracy hinge on their further exclusion. As we consider our complicity with the exclusionary landscape of academe, we might at least glimpse one facet of transformation that needs to occur: the weakening of the border between the cognitively nondisabled and the intellectually disabled—both in our conceptual and physical worlds. Confronted with radical cognitive differences, we might begin to consider how we repeatedly tie our identities, our places, and our futures to compulsory capacity. When we presume that we can dismantle our anxiety about disability with knowledge, we reassert the fantasyland of the cognitively ideal world: that we have control over our minds; that we can decide to choose the way we think; and that we can, on demand, recalibrate the way we feel. This fantasy disavows disability all over again, as it sustains the familiar and fantastic cognitively ideal self—always troublesome, always seductive.

CHAPTER 4

Rethinking Political Agency

Arendt and the Self-Advocacy Movement

A T THE 2010 ANNUAL CONFERENCE OF SABE (Self Advocates Becoming Empowered), Max Burrows, a young African American man, articulated the success and mission of the movement in his speech for SABE's vice presidency: "In Vermont, we've got sticks and we've got mountains, but there's one thing we don't have . . . and that's no institutions! [*sic*]. No sheltered workshops! And no enclaves!" Like most candidates running for office within SABE, Burrows attacked the isolating and exploitative conditions promoted by state policies for people with intellectual disabilities. Burrows's passionate speech earned lots of audience applause. Burrows urged the crowd onward: "We've still got more work to do. We've got to change attitudes!"[1]

Burrows won the vice presidency of SABE—an easy task, since he ran uncontested. But there was a palpable feel of support for him in the large banquet room in which he gave his speech. I sat at the back of the room at a table surrounded by self-advocates. Burrows's speech came after five people had described their own platform for SABE's presidency. Unlike Burrows, these candidates' speeches wandered haphazardly through points, at times needing to return to the beginning. Some shouted slogans, while others were barely audible. Burrows's speech—its linearity—was welcomed by the crowd. A man across from me at the table stared down at his plate and mumbled to no one at all, "Why isn't this guy running for president?" His question captures a tension in the self-advocacy movement itself and the capacity contract that I have described in this book: a tension between a desire to conform to the tenets of compulsory capacity to garner political legitimacy and a need to reject norms around capacity as arbitrary and harmful to people with intellectual disabilities.

Evading this tension is difficult, as the language of self-advocacy is intimately tied to cognitive capacity. Earning respect and political standing is central to the self-advocacy movement—and, indeed, democracy more broadly. For example, People First of West Virginia describes self-advocacy as "a person's ability to effectively communicate, convey, negotiate or assert his/her own interests, needs, and rights. Self-advocacy is understanding your strengths and needs, . . . knowing your legal rights and responsibilities, and communicating these to others."[2] The list of cognitive tasks embedded in self-advocacy is long: communicating, conveying, negotiating, asserting, understanding, and knowing. Moreover, People First of West Virginia assigns these tasks to individuals, as a person must gain these abilities to advocate effectively.

In the self-advocacy movement's goal of empowerment, demands for compulsory capacity surface often. Empowerment can capture many things, but most often, it refers to the idea that individuals should identify as members of an oppressed class and then use that identification as a basis for demanding rights and empowering others who are similarly situated. For example, the website of People First of Washington states, "WE ARE PEOPLE FIRST AND WE CAN SPEAK FOR OURSELVES!"[3] People First of California similarly describes its philosophy:

> People with developmental disabilities are the only people to empower other people with developmental disabilities. Only the people, who are part of a certain culture, can "empower" people of that culture; to become strong, they have to make the decisions and do the work of their movement, themselves.[4]

Making decisions, communicating the message, and acquiring a cultural identity are all cognitive tasks. Griet Roets and Dan Goodley echo this model of empowerment: "Through sharing life stories, self-advocates are able to recognize their oppressed status in the dominant discourses and institutions in which they find their selves positioned."[5] Empowerment thus encapsulates dominant liberal democratic norms of independence and autonomy and counters the profound form of powerlessness that marks the history of people with intellectual disabilities.

While these are vital tasks for self-advocates, they pose two problems. First, they exclude from self-advocacy some people with intellectual disabilities. According to Allison Carey, the self-advocacy movement is "uncomfortably silent" on the ways in which liberal norms of autonomy and competence threaten to heighten prejudice against people who are unable to attain these same abilities.[6] Second, this understanding of empowerment is too narrow, as it ignores noncognitive modes of political action. Herein lies the challenge: empowerment-as-compulsory capacity undermines the goal of empowering *all* people with intellectual disabilities.

In rethinking empowerment, I draw on an unlikely source: Hannah Arendt. Arendt's conception of action, developed in *The Human Condition*, provides us with a rich resource for resituating the focus of political empowerment from questions of subjectivity toward public action. More specifically, I use Arendt's account of politics to evaluate my observations of a self-advocacy organization gathered over a two-year period. Through Arendt's account, I began to see that both nondisabled staff members and self-advocates with intellectual and developmental disabilities offer an alternative account of empowerment. In this new model, we are focusing our attention outward—judging the physical location of advocacy practices as well as the kinds of relationships that self-advocacy groups foster—rather than measuring empowerment by an inner cognitive consciousness.

Compulsory Capacity in the Movement

In many ways, empowerment as compulsory capacity is about control: control over one's life, body, future, and political movement. Self-advocates' emphasis on control arises from the history of the self-advocacy movement, in which self-advocates have struggled to maintain their right to speak for themselves. Compared to other disability rights groups and parental advocacy groups, self-advocacy is relatively recent, with the first self-advocacy group in the United States established in 1974. In comparison, the League of the Physically Handicapped began in 1935; the National Federation of the Blind was created in 1940, and one of the first parental rights groups, The Arc, was launched in 1953.[7]

Before self-advocacy groups formed, the political landscape was marked by two waves of advocacy experts: professionals who gained credibility at the beginning of the twentieth century, and parents who began advocating in the 1950s.[8] Many self-advocacy groups were initially started collaboratively, with nondisabled staff or parents providing support.[9] Frank Bylov describes three generations in self-advocacy: the first groups that were run by professionals in segregated facilities; the second that were developed within parental organizations; and the third—"movements of empowerment"—that are run by and for people with intellectual disabilities.[10] Bylov's description of these waves as generations can be misleading, as many self-advocacy groups are intertwined with professional or parental groups.

The first self-advocacy group is credited to a group of people with intellectual disabilities in Sweden, who were part of Swedish leisure clubs that were training people with disabilities in self-governance.[11] According to Hayden and Nelis, the Swedish self-advocacy organization began in 1968, when parents involved in a parental rights organization asked people with intellectual disabilities about the kinds of changes they desired.[12] According to People First of West Virginia, in contrast, the real impetus for self-advocacy occurred when the children of the members of the Swedish parental rights group decided that the group's motto, "We speak for them," would no longer do.[13] Tensions thus exist over the origin story of the self-advocacy movement and the degree to which it was forged alongside or against parental advocacy groups. This history is in part difficult to trace, as the self-advocacy movement is less well documented than are other advocacy organizations.[14]

Over the next five years, similarly motivated organizations began to spread to Canada. Prior to this, the parental advocacy organization Canadian Association for the Mentally Retarded (CAMR) was one of the first charity organizations to reject the pity paradigm of disability. Later renamed the Canadian Association for Community Living (CACL), the organization faced internal discord in regard to a high-profile court case: a mother wanted to sterilize her developmentally disabled daughter. Parental advocates disagreed over the issue, but people with intellectual disabilities who were part of the group decided to form their own group in order to denounce sterilization policies.[15]

Self-advocates who became politically mobilized over the trial were some of the same people who would go on to found People First.[16] In 1973, a conference for people with intellectual disabilities was held in British Columbia, and a handful of staff members and residents from Oregon's Fairview Hospital and Training Center attended. A year later, on January 8, 1974, nine people met at a group home in Salem, Oregon, and decided to launch the first self-advocacy conference in the United States. According to People First of Oregon, it was also at this meeting that the name People First originated: "In the course of planning the convention, the small group of planners decided they needed a name for themselves. A number of suggestions had been made when someone said, 'I'm tired of being called retarded—we are people first.' The name People First was chosen and the People First self-advocacy movement began."[17] Later that same year, the first U.S. self-advocacy conference was held in Salem and 560 people attended.[18]

Currently, People First describes itself as a self-advocacy organization "run by and for people with disabilities" and credits itself with being the "oldest and best known" self-advocacy organization in the United States. Although People First remains a state and local organization without a national headquarters, it has an estimated seventeen thousand members. In the United States, there are over eight hundred self-advocacy chapters, and at the international level, at least forty-three countries have self-advocacy organizations, many of which are People First chapters.[19]

Tensions between parents and self-advocates continued through the 1980s. Indeed, some parental groups formed against the civil rights of people with intellectual disabilities, exemplified by the group Voice of the Retarded, which fought to preserve institutions.[20] Although most parental advocacy groups have since embraced self-determination as a goal, many of them did so in order to garner better services rather than to advance claims for civil rights.[21] More recent tensions have emerged between the neurodiversity movement—led primarily by adults with autism who see autism as a valuable human difference—and parental groups like Generation Rescue, which attribute the cause of autism to vaccinations and thus aim to promote individual recovery from autism.[22]

Additionally, neither parental advocates nor self-advocates fit fully into the larger disability rights movement, which was gaining momentum in the 1970s and 1980s.[23] Professionals and parents did not position themselves within the disability rights movement, as many of them felt that the movement was too radical and placed too much emphasis on self-determination.[24] Meanwhile, the disability rights movement was not always welcoming of people with intellectual impairments.[25]

Physically disabled activists were uneasy about adding people with mental impairments to their movement in fear that they would undermine their claims for competence and autonomy.[26] Tensions existed over the term *self-advocate* itself, with some advocates with disabilities avoiding the term in order to distance themselves from the stigma of "mental retardation."[27] In Canada, some disability activists only wanted to push for discrimination protection for people with physical disabilities, as they worried that the inclusion of people with intellectual disabilities would dilute the meaning of the law.[28] Consequently, as professionals, parents, and other disability rights activists worried about the capacities of people with intellectual disabilities, self-advocates were under more pressure to demand recognition as equally competent.

Self-advocates' desire to be seen as competent and to be given control over their own lives stems from their history of institutionalization. Some describe the total lack of autonomy and isolation in their daily lives, from going to bed, eating, dressing, and employment, to forced sterilization and harsh disciplinary techniques.[29] Because institutionalization was premised on their presumed incompetence, self-advocates demand recognition as competent.

Control also surfaces in research conducted by and about people with intellectual disabilities, in which researchers identify "achieving some level of control over their own lives" as a shared value. Researchers thus explore ways to facilitate self-advocacy practices that can foster control.[30] Stacy Nonnemacher and Linda Bambara interviewed self-advocates with intellectual disabilities and found two recurring themes when they asked people to define self-determination: "speaking out and being in charge."[31] According to one interviewee, "When 'the ball is in my court, I decide how things should be done.'"[32] Similarly, in interviews with thirteen self-advocates, Gilmartin and Slevin found that self-advocates value having control over decision making, as one participant stated, "'We decide ourselves.'"[33] Speaking up for oneself and gaining the authority to make decisions are two dominant themes across the literature on self-advocacy.

Thus, researchers argue that one of the most effective methods for empowering people with intellectual disabilities is the creation of self-advocacy groups in which members control the agenda and make key decisions.[34] Researchers find, however, that tensions over control continue to plague groups, as nondisabled group advisers often exercise undue influence on group decisions or underestimate self-advocates' abilities.[35] Similarly, self-advocates argue that professionals and service agencies threaten to co-opt empowerment by paying lip service to self-determination while refusing to displace the power hierarchies between professionals and self-advocates.[36] Consequently, scholars interested in empowering the self-advocacy movement aim to increase the political voice of individual members, build relationships between people with disabilities, and identify what type of organizational structures promote individual agency.[37] While these interventions are important, they circumvent the tension between compulsory capacity and cognitive vulnerability.

Thus, we may be reluctant to decouple empowerment from compulsory capacity not only because self-advocates value control but also because the self-advocacy movement is constantly under siege. But even in research that documents the value of control, researchers suggest that the meaning of self-advocacy remains ambiguous,[38] and that control is just one of many values that people with intellectual disabilities hold.[39] Additionally, while values such as control and autonomy are prominent in the culture of self-advocacy groups in the West, values such as community and interdependence are equally important in some non-Western self-advocacy groups.[40] Critical disability studies scholars similarly criticize the norm of sovereignty as a modernist fabrication—a mythical norm used to stigmatize people with disabilities. According to Margrit Shildrick, the sovereign self implies that we—our bodies and minds—are "under control, predictable, determinate, and above all independent in form and function."[41] Compulsory capacity thus ignores the ways in which people are vulnerable, unpredictable, and interdependent.

Moreover, when self-advocates and their allies refuse to engage with the tension of cognitive impairment and compulsory capacity, they may actually be surrendering those issues to other organizations—perhaps to the professionals that they criticize.[42] If self-advocacy aims to represent a broad spectrum of people with intellectual disabilities—which indeed it does—then it cannot circumvent the issues related to dependency, self-determination, and profound cognitive impairment. Hannah Arendt's conception of politics offers us a way to hold true to these tensions without silencing self-advocates.

An Arendtian Alternative

Using Arendt for a project on disability and democracy presents several challenges, including her division between public and private spheres, her inability to see the political dimensions of pain, and—perhaps most difficult—her characterization of speech as the marker of human life. All of these dimensions threaten to devalue people with intellectual disabilities and their experiences. But Arendt's thinking is full of contradictions, leading many theorists to "think with Arendt *against* Arendt."[43] I particularly find promise in Arendt's conception of politics as spontaneous, plural, and public action. Rethinking empowerment through these dimensions pushes us beyond compulsory capacity. My analysis is not meant to fully articulate Arendt's theory; rather, it pushes off Arendt, as a swimmer pushes off the ledge of a pool.

Arendt offers us a theory of a semisovereign subject in which "no one can know himself, for no one appears to himself as he appears to others."[44] While the traditional subject of social contract theory must conform to compulsory capacity—controlling all of her actions so they conform to her identity—the semisovereign subject welcomes spontaneous action because it reveals to herself and to others new dimensions of her identity.[45] Additionally, Arendt is uninterested in the psychological qualities that prompt people to act, arguing that they are "typical" of many of the same people and, as such, lose the quality of offering something new to the public realm.[46] More broadly, Arendt criticizes Western philosophy for attempting the impossible in the quest to "arrive at a definition of man."[47] As detailed in the chapters on Locke and Rawls, these attempts at defining always incite exclusion and limit human possibilities.

As such, Arendt critiques modern society for stifling spontaneity because it "expects from each of its members a certain kind of behavior, imposing innumerable and various rules, all of which tend to 'normalize' its members, to make them behave, to exclude spontaneous action or outstanding achievement."[48] Rather than conform to norms of democratic comportment, Arendt emphasizes the importance of bringing forth something new in the public sphere. For Arendt, we forfeit spontaneity for the false promise of sovereignty when we reduce politics to "solvable problems of cognition."[49] In contrast, Arendt's spontaneous subject encounters politics as performative and unpredictable.

Arendt's critique of sovereignty hinges on her understanding of politics as plural: that deeds and words are significant when they occur in the presence of others. For Arendt, "if it were true that sovereignty and freedom are the same, then indeed no man could be free, because sovereignty, the ideal of uncompromising self-sufficiency and mastership, is contradictory to the very condition of plurality."[50] Not only do we lack full awareness of ourselves, but the plurality of politics means that we cannot foretell the interpretation or consequences of our actions. Importantly for Arendt, "to be isolated is to be deprived of the capacity to act," whereas action always establishes a "web of human relationships."[51] To be sovereign is to be isolated and apolitical, whereas action "lies between people and [can] bind them together."[52]

Not all action, however, is political for Arendt. Going to work, or enjoying the sociability of eating and drinking together, is not political action for Arendt precisely because these activities collapse people together in their sameness.[53] Yet, as Margaret Canovan explains, understanding the precise boundaries of Arendtian political action is difficult. For instance, Canovan argues that Arendt offers unexpected examples of political action, such as Jesus of Nazareth offering forgiveness.[54] Elsewhere Arendt suggests that "action . . . always establishes relationships and therefore has an inherent tendency to force open all limitations and cut across boundaries."[55] Thinking with Arendt *against* Arendt, if eating dinner in public forges new relations and challenges entrenched ableist boundaries, then perhaps this action is political, as it "establishes relationships and creates new realities."[56]

Arendt's account of action as public is a crucial component behind the self-advocacy movement. The "true space [of politics] lies between people living together for this purpose [acting and speaking together], no matter where they happen to be."[57] Arendt's emphasis on people living together takes on new significance when compared to the isolation, segregation, and limited social network that marks the lives of people with intellectual disabilities. Although Arendt's focus on rightlessness applied to stateless people, her concerns map onto the lives of people with disabilities, as the "calamity of [disability] is not belonging to any community," not because of any innate biological inferiority but because of the history of segregation that has marked disabled people.[58]

Importantly, the public realm makes remembrance possible. For Arendt, "The privation of privacy lies in the absence of others; as far as they are concerned, private man does not appear, and therefore it is as though he did not exist."[59] This fear of disappearance is particularly salient for people with intellectual disabilities, whose life stories and histories have only recently begun to appear. Indeed, the repeated description of "out of sight, out of mind" often refers to the history of people with intellectual disabilities.

Plurality and publicity are linked for Arendt, as individual action takes on significance when undertaken before other people. "Being seen and being heard by others derive their significance from the fact that everybody sees and hears from a different position."[60] This public and plural nature of politics triggers multiple meanings from our actions, as we cannot control the ways in which others will interpret our actions, again splintering the façade of compulsory capacity.

Arendt's emphasis on action can potentially move us away from measuring individual cognitive capacity as the marker of political membership, but her emphasis on speech is troublesome. "Speechless action would no longer be action because there would no longer be an actor, and the actor, the doer of deeds, is possible only if he is at the same time the speaker of words."[61] Without speech there is no identity—no unique or distinct qualities that can usher in a new beginning.

But if we think with Arendt *against* Arendt, then we can question the ways in which the rules of speech threaten to dampen action's potential for the unexpected and the new. According to Arendt, "The fact that man is capable of action means that the unexpected can be expected from him, that he is able to perform what is infinitely improbable."[62] As self-advocates realize, speech invites categorization, and categories like "retarded" and "intellectually disabled" constrain the ways in which the identities of those being categorized can be imagined and received. Reclaiming Arendt for self-advocacy may mean that we move away from her focus on speech as revealing an individual's identity. Instead, we can consider how speech *and* action are often collaborative, undertaken *between* people with a range of capacities.[63]

Arendt's theory of action thus offers us another way to judge the efficacy of self-advocacy groups. While we should question whether self-advocacy organizations foster self-determination, we should also ask if self-advocacy groups are meeting in public, fostering relationships, and promoting spontaneous action. Living spontaneously in public with others *is* a mode of empowerment, as it powerfully contests the notion that a disabled life is not worth living. For self-advocates and allies, we need to consider empowerment—not only as an internal psychological dimension but also as an intersubjective experience between people.

When empowerment is conceptualized as control, it positions self-advocates against advisers, allies, staff, and family members. And yet researchers find that fostering trusting and encouraging relationships between staff members and self-advocates in noncongregate settings is central to promoting self-determination.[64] In the following section, I describe the self-advocacy organization I observed, arguing that if we read the events under the rubric of compulsory capacity, we will emerge dissatisfied. But if we look for empowerment through an Arendtian lens, we can see how self-advocates and allies offer us an engaging and dynamic vision of political action.

Research Methods: Grounded Theory and Narrative Inquiry

My analysis draws heavily on the qualitative research method of grounded theory. Initially articulated by Glaser and Strauss, grounded theory challenges the extreme positivism of social science inquiry that emulates the scientific method.[65] Grounded theory enabled me to make meaning out of the self-advocacy movement I observed rather than according to its explicit mission. As a political theorist, however, I did not use grounded theory to reach generalizable claims. Instead, I used grounded theory to reconceptualize key theoretical concepts. Given Arendt's own tendency to theorize from events, grounded theory is especially appropriate.[66]

I relied heavily on Kathy Charmaz's description of specific methods for grounded theorists—such as theoretical sampling and memoing—by which a researcher can simultaneously immerse herself in theoretical development while remaining self-reflexive to her role as a researcher.[67] I base my analysis on field notes, which I transcribed after attending events, as I found note taking during observations too distracting. I recorded details of observed events within twenty-four hours of attendance. If parts of my observation would occur to me later, I would transcribe these aspects in a memo. I continually reflected on my field notes through Charmaz's description of memoing—writing my reflections and then analyzing them in an iterative process.

By presenting my observations in narrative form—in which names and places are fictionalized to protect participants' identities—I offer the reader a rich descriptive account, showing how events filtered through my own perspective and how I elicited meaning from particular interactions. My integration of self-advocates' actions follows the work of scholars who share in the value of empowering people with intellectual disabilities by integrating their voices and actions within research as a way to destabilize dominant patterns of exclusion.[68] Many disability studies scholars choose life stories and interviews to capture the details of an individual's life. Narrative offers a robust picture of people's actions and can explore the relational dynamics across people both with and without disabilities.[69] Moreover, it captures Arendt's own emphasis on storytelling, as without it, the fleetingness of action would render all acts obscure.[70] By observing self-advocacy events and continually memoing on my observations, I came to reconceptualize empowerment from compulsory capacity to public spontaneity.

Observing Self-Advocates in Action

Between November 2008 and May 2010, I observed the day-to-day operations and local chapter meetings of a self-advocacy organization in the southern United States. The central office I observed employed four people across three regional offices, which served around twenty to twenty-five local chapters. Arlene, the director, described to me how the first chapter began:

> It started with a small group home that actually had seen a movie about an organization in Oregon. These people in Oregon, they were empowered; they were speaking up for themselves; they were making changes in their state, and so these people, this group of I think twelve people that lived in a group home at that time, saw this movie, and they said "we want to do that here."

Since then, the number of chapters varied, reaching a high of forty, but had since declined.

The central self-advocacy office I observed was located in an old office building, squeezed between fast-food restaurants, gas stations,

and strip malls. The lobby opened into a deserted first floor, once occupied by a carpet retailer that had abandoned its space but had left a
large billboard opposite the elevator. The one-room office was at the
end of the hall on the third floor; Arlene's desk sat at the back of the
room, partially obscured by a large bookcase and the cumbersome
computer and printer atop her desk. Empty desks surrounded Arlene,
left from another advocacy agency that disbanded when budget short-
falls made it impossible to continue advocating for its clients living in
state-run facilities. During my time volunteering, the organization
faced its own budget crisis. Although the state legislature renewed its
grant, it delayed disbursing the funds, causing Arlene to forgo her sala-
ry for four months and to eventually lay off the eastern coordinator.

Beyond economic hardships, the agencies that served members
threatened to hamper the effectiveness of the advocacy groups, as Arlene's goal of coordinating meetings and events hinged on agencies'
willingness to cooperate. For instance, out of the twenty or so local
chapters, only one was able to meet in public; the rest gathered in the
residential homes or sheltered workshops where the members lived
and worked. When I asked Arlene to explain this discrepancy, she
sighed and explained:

> Actually we would like all of them to be meeting out in the
> community, but for one reason or another, I think for most of
> them if we tried to meet out in the community they wouldn't
> get there, just for transportation issues, so, for convenience
> sake we meet in the agencies a lot of time, and there are some
> agencies that are willing to work, and get their people out to
> different places, but for the most part, we do good just to get
> them to let us come in there.

She then laughed. On the one hand, Arlene attributed the difficulties
of meeting in public to issues of transportation, but the end of her statement suggested that there is more to agencies' resistance. In fact, research
shows that although service providers may support disability rights aims
of self-determination and social inclusion in their mission statements,
in practice, staff may operate independent of these goals, organizing
work around their own preferences and maintaining the segregation of
people with intellectual disabilities.[71]

As my relationship with Arlene grew, I learned that her laughter was a common response to exasperation. In this case, her laughter suggested the kinds of difficulties that people with intellectual disabilities face in seemingly simple activities, like meeting in public. The Fellowship Group—the only chapter to meet in public—thus occupied a unique position among the twenty-plus groups across the state. As I detail in my narrative in the next section, the Fellowship Group offers us a new model of empowerment, focused on how people act in the world in the presence of others.

Sovereignty Surfacing and Sputtering

The Fellowship Group chapter met monthly at a local buffet restaurant. On the night I attended, the group was seated in the banquet room—separate but still visible to other patrons. Servers and patrons often passed through the swinging doors going back and forth to the buffet. Around thirty-five people were scattered across the eleven tables in the room. It was difficult for me to identify staff from self-advocates. Visible markers—like wearing helmets or needing assistance with eating—provided some cues, but more frequently, I suspected that someone might have an intellectual disability once people began to talk with each other. Most in attendance were African American and male; eight were white and thirteen were women, including Arlene. Race was particularly salient, in part because the self-advocacy organization was located in the southern portion of the United States, and it marked different levels of privilege in the meeting. Both advisers of the meeting were white, as were the professionals. Most of the people with disabilities and support staff, in contrast, were African American. Whereas the servers working in the restaurant were African American, all other patrons were white.

Gender was also significant. Although my estimates are imprecise, twelve men were self-advocates, leaving around six or seven male employees. Among the women, about eight were staff. Most of the women with disabilities, all except one, sat at a corner table (along with female employees working with them). Employees behaved in a variety of roles: some were more supervisory, overseeing the behavior of members directly; others were involved in the organizational structure of the self-advocacy group; and others seemed to fill the role of friend. Employees more concerned with overseeing the actions of people with disabilities balanced different tasks: helping members get food and utensils, and chaperoning members to the bathroom and outside to smoke. In general, women staff members were more likely to perform work around food, which correlates with research that finds women staff members to be more care oriented than their male colleagues.[72] Three of the women worked with the more severely disabled individuals—and by "severe" I mean individuals whose intellectual disability was compounded with some sort of physical disability (made evident by a person being in a wheelchair, having difficulty manipulating utensils, wearing a protective helmet, or appearing to be nonverbal). Male employees more often seemed to fill the role of friend and audience—in part because most of the clients are men as well, but also because gendered dynamics of the social contract—which associate women with the private realm and dependency needs—continues to inform nondisabled and disabled interactions.[73]

The evening had two portions: the monthly business meeting occupied the first thirty minutes, which was then followed by dinner and fellowship. These two portions of the meeting roughly map onto two different models of empowerment: one that enforces compulsory capacity and an Arendtian alternative that privileges collective spontaneous action in public.

During the business meeting, nondisabled staff members and advisers steered the agenda. I sat across from Mason, who chaired the meeting. Mason was a young black man who wore his hat toward the back of his head so that all I could see was the underside of the cap's bill. He was soft spoken and often cut off the end of his words, making his speech difficult to understand. Mason sat next to Bobby, an older white man and an adviser, who helped Mason move through the agenda. Bobby always asked, "Do you remember what's next?" Mason seldom remembered, and so Bobby pointed to each line, explaining to Mason what to say. "Now ask if anyone has any new business." "New . . . ," Mason responded, but then failed to finish the sentence. "New business," encouraged Bobby.

The first item of business was calling the roll, meaning that Mason pointed to every person in the room, asking "Wassuhnaaa" and waiting for a response. This was a relatively easy task at our table, where Mason sat, but his voice was so soft that many people to the side did not hear him. This did not bother Mason, as he continued pointing at individuals and asking their names, even if that person did not look at him. In this way, he seemed oblivious to the idea that if people did not realize he was pointing at them, they would not answer. However, Mason never raised his voice, nor did he make any other type of command to alert a table he was calling their roll. In fact, his humorous exasperation suggested that he attributed the fault entirely to others. In these cases, Bobby or someone else called attention to the person Mason was pointing toward. At the back table with the women, a female employee introduced the others by name; other than that, most people introduced themselves.

After the roll call, a staff member slowly read the old minutes. Mostly we heard names, as the previous month's roll call provided the bulwark of the minutes. Afterward, Mason asked Betty to give the treasurer's report. The treasurer's report unfolded like the old game of telephone: first, a supervisor whispered the number to Betty's attendant, who then whispered it to Betty, who then barked out in a deep voice: "Fifty-one dollars!" The attendant audibly whispered to Betty again, "and seventy-one cents." But this time Betty's voice was softer, with most of the syllables inaudible, so that all I heard was "Sevvvsssss." We may read these interactions centering on Mason and Betty positively, interpreting advisers and staff as actively encouraging their participation, or we may be less sanguine and accord professionals too much control over self-advocates' behaviors.

During old business, Arlene and Bobby stated that last month's meeting, during which a woman came in to talk about voting, was a real success. Here, we see traditional forms of democratic mobilization and citizenship that buoys empowerment as compulsory capacity. This meeting was just two days after the 2008 presidential election, and Arlene asked how many people had voted. Five or six people raised their hand. They agreed that last month's mobilization efforts went well, that they should do it again, and that several people had registered and voted for the first time.

Uneven power dynamics between advisers, staff, and members re-emerged around new business. Arlene made a proposal for next month's meeting: rather than meet at the restaurant for dinner, the group could have a Christmas party at the community center. Instead of dinner, they could have a dance with a DJ and have some snacks, and possibly some sandwiches, with an admission charge of ten dollars. When Arlene mentioned *dance*, Mason pumped his fist in the air, exclaiming, "Yeah, a dance!" Questions from staff members were answered, and the vote for the dance was about to begin, but a black man with a goatee sitting in the corner in a white netted ball cap asked if having a dance meant that they could not meet for dinner at the buffet restaurant. He was concerned with whether the agency would be notified beforehand. I did not know if this man had a disability or not. He was given an answer but remained dissatisfied. He asked the same question again and was once more assured. The group tried to vote, but the meeting became disordered. First Mason asked people who were in favor of the dance to raise their hands, but only a few people assented. Bobby and Arlene then told Mason to ask instead if anyone opposed the dance. This time, no one said anything, and the measure passed. When the dance passed, several men started talking excitedly about a possible "dance-off." Sue, another staff member, told them to start practicing and to remember their dancing shoes. Meanwhile, the concerned man from the corner again asked if it meant they would not be having dinner at the buffet restaurant; Arlene explained to him the vote, and the meeting moved on. But later in the evening, I overheard the man talking to other staff members, leaning on their table, asking them questions about the dance.

When the meeting seemed about to adjourn, Bobby reminded Mason to ask a final time, "Any new business?" Behind me, a man sitting at a table raised his hand. Bobby pointed this out to Mason, who then gave the floor to the man. "Yeah, I got new business," he said loudly, "Barack Obama is our new president!" Suddenly, people laughed, clapped, and hollered in delight, thus giving the closing of the meeting an exuberant edge.

In many ways, we see traditional accounts of empowerment: interest in voting in the recent presidential election, the different appointed officers, and the protocol of the meeting. However, in other ways, members of the Fellowship Group failed to achieve sufficient compulsory capacity to achieve requisite levels of empowerment. Mason was unable to lead the meeting and seemed to mimic the words of Bobby. Nondisabled advisers and staff held most of the discussion of new business. We might ask, referring back to our traditional model of empowerment, if members understood themselves as political, if they

understood their rights and responsibilities, and if they situated themselves within a broader movement of disability rights activism. The
Fellowship Group seemed steered by a few cognitively able advisers
and staff members, surrounded by passive support staff and disabled
clients—a division that was marked by race. The meeting, however,
constituted a relatively short part of the evening; the dinner and fellowship that followed consumed the rest of the night.

Significantly, this portion of the evening occurred once the advisers
left. As people finished dinner, Arlene and Bobby prepared to leave.
Sue reprimanded them, "You can't leave your guest!" Arlene turned
back to me, and I encouraged her to go, reassuring her that I was okay.
As they left, Arlene invited me to their upcoming December dance.
With the two paid employees of People First gone and dinner mostly
eaten, a new form of politics emerged.

Spontaneity Plural and Public

The room grew louder, including the staff. With the absence of advisers, people began to move around the room, and the hierarchies of authority—so clear during the meeting—seemed to relax. Mason moved
to another table behind me with a young man whom I assumed to be
an employee because, like other staff members, he wore an ID card. He
laughed a lot and caused Mason to laugh a lot as well. This pattern of
movement and laughter then traveled throughout the rest of the room
as more people finished eating, left their seats, and visited one another.
Like Arendt's description of action, this portion of the meeting aimed
at promoting togetherness.

The talk of the upcoming dance consumed one table, with a man
loudly boasting that he was "the best dancer in the room." Women staff
members teased him to dance, but he protested: he would not dance
without his dancing shoes and without music. Across the room, a
young slender man wearing all black and a black cap took up the challenge. Positioning himself at the center of the room, he faced a group of
male staff members who loudly encouraged people to dance. The slender man stood and faced the taunting crowd, perfectly still for a moment, but then his body slowly slid into dance. With his right hand on
his chest, his feet moved in a series of stationary steps. He wrapped his

left foot around his right and gave a smooth and slow pirouette. Returning to his initial position of facing the male crowd, he slid the thumb and finger of his left hand across the brim of his hat, signaling his big finale. The crowd erupted! Women and men cheered as he turned and walked back to his table.

Amid much laughing and clapping, the crowd turned their attention to the man who forgot his dancing shoes. "Show us your moves! Just one!" He protested, but before he had the chance to dance, the man in all black returned to his position and began dancing again, this time incorporating more moves from his body. Another man, who had been sitting quietly in the corner, stood up. Stan, who introduced himself to me earlier in the evening, was a short middle-aged white man, wearing a fanny pack under his round belly and a permanent pinched smile on his face. Stan stationed himself and controlled the room's attention. He copied the young man's moves: holding his arms bent close to his waist, he turned in a slow circle, smiling the entire time. At the end of the rotation, the people in the room, including myself this time, cheered and laughed. Stan sat down, but his dance triggered more opportunities of performance as more and more people began to dance: a young man in blue, Mason, and the man in black. Each was its own performance, as no one danced at the same time. Dancing encapsulates Arendt's description of political action: it is public, spontaneous, and plural. It also demonstrates a way in which people can express themselves without speech.

Around this time, a woman leaned over to me across the aisle and said, "When the meeting's over, they like to have fun!" Though her use of "they" prickled of paternalism, it was also misleading. The fun was contagious, as enjoyment spread across clients, employees, and even the servers who bustled in and out of the room. Beside me, a table of staff and self-advocates surpassed all others in their boisterous fun and good-natured teasing. When Liz, a white female professional, got up to get dessert, a waiter grabbed her silverware. The women and men at the table waited, holding back their giggles, and watched Liz pile her plate with dessert, not realizing that the waiter had taken her fork and spoon. When she returned, they all laughed. Liz smiled and simply unrolled the set of utensils by the empty chair beside her.

This small and silly interaction in fact shows the fluidity of power hierarchies, as a nondisabled professional (Liz wore a business suit)

became the target of teasing. Teasing—around either Liz or the danc-
ers—occurred across race, gender, and status, as staff members teased
self-advocates and self-advocates teased staff. Teasing shares Arendt's
dimensions of action: it occurs between people in public, and it is spontaneous. Like dancing, it joyfully plays with power as it knits people together in bonds of reciprocity.[74]

As the room grew louder and men continued to dance, I looked
through the glass at a white couple seated at a booth on the other side
of the restaurant. They stared with blank faces into our room, quietly
looking on to the fun. I wondered what they thought, what they saw:
Did they realize that the men dancing were intellectually disabled?
Would it have made a difference? Or did they perceive the self-advocacy
activities not through the lens of disability but through the narrative of
race? Arendt helps us here, too, as she argues that the consequences of
action are unknowable and unpredictable.

By the end of the evening, patrol of behavior had ceased, until the
young man in black began to dance again, this time facing me, only a
foot away. As his hips began to move back and forth, a staff member in-
terjected, "That's enough. Go sit back down." He took a few steps to his
table, but before he sat down, he turned around and resumed his position, now turned the other way toward the men. He gave the same hip-
shaking move, but without reproach. Some part of me—my whiteness, gender, or outsider status—triggered control in an otherwise
spontaneous climate.

Around this time, the people at the boisterous table beside me prepared to leave. The "best dancer" had still not shown us any moves. Together the four of them stood in front of Liz's table and talked.

"Tell them what you've been doing," said a staff member.

"Ka-ra-tay," the man said, slowly with a smile, emphasizing the "tay"
at the end of the sentence.

"Show us some moves."

The man at first stood still, as if he would refuse this too, but then his
right arm stabbed sidewise into the air. The women laughed. Once they
left, I lingered for a few minutes and then said good-bye to Liz. Like
Arlene, she invited me to attend the Christmas party and to "bring
some friends."

As I made my way to the exit, the group of four still talked about ka-
ra-tay. The women teased the man to show more moves, and in the

middle of the restaurant, he stopped, bent his back to the floor, and—kick!—he stabbed the air with his right leg. More laughter thundered out as we all made our way out the door. I waved good-bye as I walked toward my car while people still laughed and practiced ka-ra-tay. For me, watching self-advocates powerfully kick the air seemed a fitting finale to the evening, a sharp kick in the face to any ableist stares that may have lurked in the corners of the restaurant.

Despite my enjoyment of the evening, I initially worried about the efficacy of the Fellowship Group. My expectations had been forged through observations of national conferences in which participation was more formal, organized, and plainly legible within a sovereign model of liberal political identity. The Fellowship Group lacked many of these markers of political advocacy: it seemed disorganized, controlled by able-minded advisers, and more interested in social connections than political transformation.

We see, however, all dimensions of Arendtian action as public, plural, and spontaneous. Together, staff members and self-advocates challenged norms of compulsory capacity, and they did so in public, in the presence of other restaurant patrons who had no expectation of sharing their dinner with self-advocates. Though difficult to measure, this portion of the evening *felt* empowering. As my involvement with People First continued—volunteering in the office, facilitating other chapter meetings, and organizing events—I began to realize the fullness of the Fellowship Group's success.

Understanding this success requires an appreciation of the difficulties involved in coordinating self-advocacy events in the region, some of which I learned from the December dance, the event so anticipated during November's meeting. The dance was held at a local community center and, due to the center's calendar, could not be held on a Thursday—the usual day of the monthly meetings. When I arrived, many of the people from November's meeting were missing. According to Arlene, many of the agencies decided to forgo the dance due to the change in time and location. Dancing in a low-lit back room of the community center—without many of the members and without an audience like the restaurant afforded—I started to understand why one man had mounted so much resistance at the November meeting. Poorly attended with no outsiders as an audience, the dance lacked the enthusiastic energy of the regular monthly meeting.

The conspicuous absence of people with intellectual disabilities from events planned around their presence became a recurrent theme in my observations. In March 2010, I attended the annual spring conference: an event initially started by self-advocates as a way to counteract the encroaching dominance of nondisabled professionals at other events. Nondisabled professionals, however, engulfed the attendance and proceedings, leaving self-advocate organizers feeling like tokens at their own creation. The last panel, "Self-Advocates Speak Up!," was the only panel organized by and for self-advocates; it was meant to rally support and empower members, but only ten people showed up: four self-advocates, three paid advisers, me, and my two children. Sitting around empty tables, the gifts that self-advocates opened did little to cheer the advisers. Likewise, the Roll-a-thon event I helped organize in May 2009 had roughly fifteen attendees. Four of us were employees or volunteers; the rest were members of our families. Not one unpaid member attended.

Other than the Fellowship Group meetings, I also attended chapter meetings held in a local sheltered workshop. By going to the workshop, Arlene averted some of the difficulties of transportation, but the spontaneity and plurality that had been so evident at the Fellowship Group meeting was entirely absent. Staff members did most of the talking; members, many of them nonverbal, generally acquiesced with any of Arlene's suggestions. I began to realize why meeting in public for dinner was so crucial: by altering the location, the Fellowship Group helped shift the general pattern of power between members and staff. Eating dinner together—rather than the usual practice of staff monitoring the eating of clients—helped alleviate the constant sense of surveillance pervasive in group homes, which undermines reciprocity.[75]

These lackluster events clearly point to the near or total absence of people with intellectual disabilities as a significant obstacle to self-advocacy. The hidden or private nature of these events echo Arendt's fear of the fate of obscurity in which people "'pass away leaving no trace that they have existed.'"[76] Having only observed one regional self-advocacy office, I cannot offer insight as to how widespread these difficulties are to the national self-advocacy movement. My point is not to mark the failures of this struggling self-advocacy office but to highlight the success of the Fellowship Group in its ability to gather people together for spontaneous action.

Arendt gives us a way to value the success of the Fellowship Group, as well as a way to want more from traditional models of empowerment. Rather than a state of mind, empowerment is a way of acting in the world with others. This fuller account of empowerment already inheres in the self-advocacy movement, as practiced by the Fellowship Group, and Arendt gives us a way to articulate it.

Conclusion: The Subject of Politics and Disability Studies

Demanding that self-advocates cultivate compulsory capacity disqualifies some people with intellectual disabilities from self-advocacy group membership and fails to capture the richness of self-advocates' political action. Revising our idea of empowerment more accurately encompasses all people with intellectual disabilities *and* better reflects the actual activities and struggles of self-advocacy groups. Empowering people in traditional sovereign modes of political subjectivity will remain essential in a liberal democratic polity, but we can also recognize and value other modes of political participation.

Understanding politics through the lens of spontaneity provides a way for us to value action outside the dominant lens of identity politics. In scholarship around disability and performance, scholars often emphasize how performers self-consciously challenge ableist stereotypes and are self-reflexive about their roles as performers. Through this lens, dancing at a buffet restaurant lacks political resistance unless the dancer self-consciously understands his action as political. In contrast, nondisabled artists who collaborate with people with intellectual disabilities emphasize how people with intellectual disabilities perform art spontaneously.[77]

Additionally, revising our understanding of political subjectivity and action promises to push the field of disability studies to be more critical of itself as an emancipatory project. Lennard Davis recently argued in the *Chronicle of Higher Education* that disability remains peripheral to academe because it contradicts "the neoliberal belief in the free and autonomous subject."[78] As such, people with disabilities jeopardize a fictive regime that idealizes our capacity of control. Critical disability studies scholars thus seem perched to erode these stubborn liberal myths—or perhaps not. According to Davis, "in disability studies, there has been a cherished belief that if we work long and hard enough in the academic arena, we will end up convincing other identities that disability is a real identity, on a par with the more recognized ones." But should we measure success by how well disability maps onto other identities—race, sex, class, and gender—and how well disability politics follows the same path as identity politics?

Here, too, we glimpse the familiar countenance of control as contained in the political subjectivity of identity politics. Anne Mollow argues that critical disability scholars—including Davis—promote an "excessive or insufficiently critical reliance upon identity" and, by extension, neoliberal identity politics.[79] Mollow rightly worries that the discipline will neglect issues of class and difference, but she fails to add that this model of identity—which grounds politics in the recognition of oneself as a member of an oppressed class—directly disempowers some people with more profound forms of cognitive impairment, as it divests them of any capacity for political action.

Thinking with Arendt (against Arendt) invites us to move the space of the political from a self-conscious identity to the space "in-between" us and the ways in which action invites a relationship between people. Arendt's theory of action offers us an alternative wherein we can jettison the fantasy of the fully sovereign subject while retaining a rich theory of democratic participation. Of course, my use of Arendt is highly selective, and much remains in her work to digest for a project on disability and democracy. Additionally, my understanding of the Fellowship Group and my own role in that understanding remain problematic. First, how members understand themselves and how they value self-advocacy remain open questions; my observations give us no insight. Moreover, signs of my own ableist and race privilege are evident in my narrative analysis. As I reread the story I have written, I become more aware of the fact that I knew the names of the white professionals and advisers but not most of the members—even the members who spoke during the meeting. Why did I not transcribe or remember their names? I could rewrite the narrative to make my lack of knowledge invisible—to try to disassociate myself from my race and ableist privilege. But I choose to leave it intact—an unwanted signature to the racial capacity contract.

As such, this is an imperfect beginning, but as Arendt pushes us to see, human action is distinct because of its ability to forge new beginnings. For Arendt, "It is in the nature of beginning that something new is started which cannot be expected from whatever may have happened before."[80] No doubt, shirking compulsory capacity is extremely difficult because it thoroughly saturates our discursive terrain. Grounded theory offers scholars a methodological way forward, as it begins with lived experience to generate theory. Studying the self-advocacy movement promises to launch new beginnings—if we begin thinking and acting spontaneously together.

CHAPTER 5

Self-Advocates and
Allies Becoming Empowered

WHEN I MET CHARLES at the self-advocacy meeting that I described in the introduction, I was skeptical that he and the self-advocacy group of which he was a part could offer new insight into the relationship between disability and democratic theory. At the time, I could not see how our shared dinner offered new possibilities for freedom. My observations that evening yielded few examples of political agency as traditionally conceptualized in scholarship, which emphasize control, autonomy, and rationality. But when my adult brother with autism moved into a state-run facility for people with intellectual disabilities three months after I met Charles, freedom began to look a lot different to me. Like many other aging caregivers in the United States, my parents could no longer care for him in their own home. His new home houses over one hundred people with intellectual and related developmental disabilities. The facility sits on the outskirts of town, and town residents refer to it as "the old state hospital." My brother's housemates include sixteen other adults, placed together because of the severity of their intellectual disabilities, exemplified by their shared and total lack of language.

My understanding of my conversation with Charles and the broader self-advocacy movement—its underlying questions about politics and my own persistent anxiety—thus unfolded as I began visiting my brother in his new institutionalized environment. I spent most of my childhood learning to interpret my brother's grunts, gestures, and twirls. Novel to me—and anxiety inducing—was the combined inarticulate sounds, jerky movements, screaming, moaning, and hand waving of the fifteen other men he lived with. Like Ellis and Bochner describe in their work on autoethnography mentioned in the introduction, these personal experiences filtered the observations I gathered, the theoretical paradigms I examined, and the analyses I pursued.[1] Throughout the research process, I often returned to personal experiences as a way to think through theoretical challenges. As Kittay poignantly points out, the personal is philosophical is political.[2]

It is unsurprising, therefore, that at the same time my brother's life disappeared from the public sphere, I began to see the political and theoretical import of living and acting *in* public. The more time I spent in his new home—cut off from the community—the more I began to appreciate the radical nature of Charles having dinner in public. Charles's slow and deliberate counting of his Cokes took on new meaning, as my brother's new institutional guardians banned caffeine from his diet, despite his preference for soda. The laughter and fellowship between staff and people with disabilities that I observed around Charles echoed against the silence of my brother's new home, as staff members' tasks and paperwork left little time to interact socially. Like the behavior at many other group homes for people with severe intellectual disabilities, interactions between staff and residents centered on functional and instructional commands.[3] Rather than taking part in spontaneous fun, staff spend much of their time filling out daily reports—as bureaucratic regulations seem more pressing than the emotional needs of residents. My brother's life thus made apparent the ways in which the personal is political, as his everyday practices—such as eating, drinking, sleeping, and being with other people—became measured, patrolled, and regimented.

In truth, however, I made the connection between Charles and my brother quite late. As I extolled the power of eating and meeting in public for self-advocates and allies, I realized that I had seldom appeared in public with my brother at all. Harlan Hahn, a leader in the disability rights movement and disability studies, once joked that people with disabilities were a cultural minority because they, like other minorities, shared a cultural diet: fast-food drive-throughs.[4] Drive-throughs sidestepped the difficulties of physical and social barriers. Eating and living in private—due to physical and stigmatizing barriers—has defined what it has meant to be disabled. Being disabled *and* public can change what it means to be disabled and, at the same time, change the dynamics of the public—as a physical and political space.[5]

Self-advocates can help us reenvision this inclusive future. In this conclusion, I draw on observations of self-advocates at a national conference, showing how they subvert compulsory capacity. As they work against domination, they also experience moments of acquiescence to the faith in cognitive capability as the foundation for political membership and a solvent for ableist oppression. I offer three tools that self-advocates use to resist compulsory capacity and build democratic capacity contracts: alliance, humor, and dance. These tools offer us ways to work within and through our anxiety—an anxiety stemming not from some essential component of disability but from our lack of experience in communicating across radical differences in cognitive capacity.

Self-Advocates Being Empowered

In September 2010, self-advocates and their allies gathered in Kansas City, Missouri, for the Self Advocates Becoming Empowered (SABE) four-day national conference. The 2010 conference theme, "Jazz It Up: Celebrating 20 Years of Self Advocates Becoming Empowered," commemorated the twenty-year anniversaries of the Americans with Disabilities Act and the founding of SABE in 1990. SABE is the first national self-advocacy organization, and it began to take shape at the First North American People First Conference in 1990. A year later, eight hundred self-advocates attended the second annual conference, and what would become SABE took on more shape.[6] Since then, SABE convenes every two years to elect eighteen board members representing nine regions in the United States.

Unlike People First, which developed alongside parental groups and service providers, SABE has positioned itself within the disability rights movement.[7] SABE's mission is to "ensure that people with disabilities are treated as equals and that they are given the same decisions, choices, rights, responsibilities, and chances to speak up to empower themselves; opportunities to make new friends; and to learn from their mistakes."[8] SABE's goals include eliminating institutions and sheltered workshops, creating equal employment opportunities for people with disabilities, making transportation systems more accessible, and educating disabled and nondisabled people about disability issues.[9] Nondisabled people can join SABE, but as nonvoting members only.

I was skeptical upon arrival in Kansas City: Would this conference attract people with disabilities and entrust them with political agency?

Between 2005 and 2010, I attended multiple conferences and work-shops convened around disability rights, organized for professionals, aca-demics, family members of people with disabilities, and advocates. At these events, people with intellectual disabilities played important but minor roles. While they often provided emotionally charged narratives, documenting harrowing stories of institutional abuse and their own courageous political activism, the actual agendas and panels of confer-ences were plainly orchestrated and staffed by nondisabled profession-als. If self-advocates offered the best testimony, nondisabled experts controlled when and how that testimony would fit into a larger frame-work of disability-related issues.

Self-advocates at SABE, however, disproved my low expectations, as they dominated the agenda and swarmed the hotel. Indeed, for the last ten years, SABE's conference has attracted more self-advocates than any other gathering in the United States. All kinds of disabilities were repre-sented, discernible through various physical signs: power wheelchairs, protective helmets, tremulous limbs, personal attendants, translators, sunglasses, and hearing aids. I recognized several self-advocates from prior conferences: Ari Ne'eman, founding president of the Autistic Self Advocacy Network; Victor Robinson, from Project ACTION in Wash-ington, D.C.; and Julie Petty, former president of SABE. Spotting famil-iar self-advocacy leaders was only a small part of my enjoyment. More thrilling was watching hundreds of self-advocates infiltrate all parts of the hotel: catching up over coffee in the lobby, overfilling the elevators with wheelchairs, and lounging on couches in hallways. At one point, I over-head a man complaining to the hotel staff that people in wheelchairs were slowing down the elevators—a testament to self-advocates' dom-inating presence and an odd subversion of whom accessibility features are meant to serve.

Like other advocacy efforts analyzed in chapter 4, SABE's self-advocates attack the presumably erroneous charge of cognitive incom-petence as a way to gain political membership. By making these claims, SABE signs on to the normalizing capacity contract, along with its ex-clusions. But SABE's self-advocates and allies also challenge compulsory capacity and enact democratic capacity contracts through alliance, humor, and dance. These tools show us how self-advocates and allies mobilize amid ableist anxiety. Caution is warranted, however, as these tools can normalize human behavior and enforce compulsory capacity.

Practicing Alliance: Mobilizing across Anxiety

Fundamental to social contract theory is the idea of cohesion: that the contract binds us together and, once bound together, we emerge anew with increased power. Similarly, the domination capacity contract highlights all those who fail to comply with compulsory capacity, but the solidarity capacity contract shifts our attention to the ways in which the contract is not an act of closure but a practice, as we imperfectly aim to understand our interconnected political aims. Self-advocates offer us a way to understand the democratic capacity contract as *practicing alliance*. Disability studies scholar and activist Paul Longmore describes how disability offers a set of alternative values around alliance, inviting "not independence but interdependence, not functional separateness but personal connection, not physical autonomy but human community."[10] Practicing alliance allows self-advocates and allies to navigate new pathways in political participation, resisting demands for compulsory capacity and paternalism.[11]

My understanding of the capacity contract as practicing alliance draws on Christine Keating's postcolonial sexual contract.[12] Forging connections of nondomination is key to Keating's revival of the contract, as it enables differently positioned groups to mobilize together to subvert domination. Although nondomination is a vital element to the democratic capacity contract, self-advocates and allies make us aware of the importance of struggle amid inequality, as participants renegotiate capacity contracts.

Practicing alliance also draws on the work of Margaret Price, who sees the value of nondisabled people becoming allies to people with disabilities even as she resists the idea that allies are necessarily knowledgeable. For Price, talk about allies too often operates at the level of intention and having the right mind-set. Instead, she notes, "I don't think we talk enough about our mistakes—what it means to make a mistake that stems from privilege or in some way reaffirms one's privilege."[13] Price prefers practicing alliance, as it makes evident the ways in which allies make mistakes.

This section focuses on the alliance between two people at SABE, Vicki and Chester, whose relationship demonstrates how we can practice alliance. In this location, filled with all kinds of people with all ranges of abilities and multiple listeners, negotiating action was collaborative, dynamic, and—at times—fumbling. But faltering did not mean failure; sometimes it meant more patience, or the need for interpretation, or someone to interject a suggestion.

Chester was the outgoing president of SABE in 2010. He is African American, plays the saxophone, is blind, and wears dark sunglasses. With his humor, Chester turned the tedious nomination of candidates lively; he hosted most of the conference's main events, which were held in an overcrowded ballroom; he filled in vacancies in seminar sessions when needed; and he acted as a judge during one event's role-play. Vicki is a middle-aged white woman, who has been involved in SABE for years as an ally. I overheard several self-advocates voice their respect for Vicki. As an ally, she was both an assistant and an agent during the conference, and thus moved in and out of different roles that required varying levels of support.[14] The relationship between allies and self-advocates is challenging, as allies must resist ableist habits of taking over the activities of the people with intellectual disabilities.[15]

In some activities, Chester required assistance, but often in different ways and different degrees. Vicki served in this capacity. Often standing slightly behind Chester and to his left, Vicki assisted Chester in orchestrating the events. With her body, she directed Chester in the right direction so he could correctly face a hand raised in the audience or the person approaching the stage. Vicki often whispered in Chester's ear, and several times they would quietly hold a quick conversation before moving on to a new activity. Hence, they publicly negotiated their coordination, showing us how practicing alliance requires participants to pause and check with each other before moving forward. For Sandhal and Auslinger, Chester and Vicki engage in "cooperative communication tactics that muddle the boundaries between individual performers and between actors and audience."[16] Vicki was also careful not to allow her privilege to overshadow Chester. When Chester called on the audience to articulate their concerns, Vicki roved about the ballroom floor with a microphone, occasionally calling out, "How many more, Chester?"

The relationship between Chester and Vicki is unique, as I also observed at SABE nondisabled allies steering action, patrolling the behaviors of people with disabilities, and choosing efficient operations rather than thick alliance—the latter of which requires attentiveness and deep knowledge of each other.[17] Practicing alliance takes time—time to develop careful attentiveness and more procedural time, as negotiating action becomes a part of the procedure. This extra time and displacement of efficiency was evident during the Fellowship Group, as Bobby and Mason slowly made their way through the agenda and a series of staff helped Betty report the treasury amount. On first interpretation, I assumed that participants underwent these awkward maneuverings to mimic autonomy, as if the coordinated fumbling of the meeting was a ruse of compulsory capacity. But within this larger framework of disruption to the capacity contract, we see these maneuverings as a way to undercut abled norms of communication.

Vicki and Chester exemplify practicing alliance because their alliance is not error-proof. For example, during the final ceremony, Chester and Vicki gave out awards. At one point, Vicki handed Chester a plaque to give one of the awardees. Chester looked down at the plaque: "Thank you for your service . . . Wait a minute! I can't read this! I'm blind!" Vicki took the microphone and read instead. At another time, a candidate running for office came to the stage to make a speech. Navigating to the front of the room took time in his large motorized wheelchair. Once on the stage, Vicki held the microphone while he very slowly said, "AHHH WIIIII WUHHHH HUUUU." Vicki mistranslated: "Brian says he would like to be your secretary." "No, he didn't!" yelled a woman from the audience. "He said he wants to work hard!" Quickly another person ran to the stage to better translate Brian's speech. Disability thus challenges the ways in which we think of the solitary orator delivering a speech to a passive audience. Instead, the speaker and audience form an alliance, in which both become active participants in crafting speech.[18] Making mistakes in public and then disrupting activities to correct these mistakes is a vital component of practicing alliance—a moment in which we renegotiate the terms of the democratic capacity contract. By negotiating power in public, SABE resists "camouflaging" power imbalances between allies and self-advocates—a trend in which allies give lip service to people-first logic but wield most of the decision-making power.[19]

Similarly, the Fellowship Group in chapter 4 revealed a wide array of disabled needs as well as a diverse set of people to attend to those needs. By displaying a diversity of disabilities that were in fact not always visible, the attendees destabilized a strict binary between the abled and the disabled. Of course, the activities of that evening did not entirely disrupt categorization. Indeed, women staff members were more likely to attend more severely disabled members. Though not ideal, People First nevertheless provides a window into imagining an alternative future in which the relationship between people is dynamic rather than static. We might think about ways that members can better promote the dynamic movement and displacement of staff, advisers, and self-advocates. We can imagine an evening or series of evenings in which members shift roles and exchange obligations as a way to disrupt the strict and opposing categories of "abled" and "disabled."

Practicing alliance is important for both sides of the capacity contract. On the one hand, the capacity contract poses risks for the ways in which it enables domination, as the most able are given power over the less able. Alliance is a way in which the more able confiscate the standing of people with disabilities, or a way for nondisabled "allies" to instill their own sets of values on the self-advocacy movement. Here, the domination capacity contract deploys alliance to enforce compulsory capacity. On the other hand, SABE's dynamic role reversals dislodge the normalizing edge of the capacity contract's dichotomy between persons and subpersons. As a democratic capacity-building tool, alliance enables people to participate together when they may not have been able to do so on their own. As a flexible device, the capacity contract sees the ways in which different people can contribute to politics by drawing on different capacities, whether those capacities are in leading a banquet dinner's events, listening attentively for mistranslated speech, helping someone navigate an overcrowded hallway, piling food onto a plate, or laughing at a joke. Laughter, as I show in the next section, helps make practicing alliance possible.

Humor: Revealing and Suspending Anxiety

Humor is another tool employed by SABE that challenges our anxiety, promotes relationships, and troubles the norms of compulsory capacity for disabled and nondisabled people alike. Research suggests that humor can reduce stigma toward people with disabilities.[20] Researchers also find that humor is one of the dominant patterns of positive social interaction between people with severe intellectual disabilities, and those without disabilities.[21] Humor reveals and, at times, alleviates anxiety, thus making relationships between nondisabled and disabled people more possible.[22] Humor is a political tool that we can use to build group solidarity, dispel stereotypes, and transgress oppressive norms.

At SABE's national conference, self-advocates and allies informally used humor, but it was also a formal part of the agenda, as the last dinner event was a performance by a disabled comedian whose humor exposed disabling societal barriers. Disability scholar Albrecht refers to this as "crip humor," which helps constitute the audience as a subculture with a shared identity.[23] By integrating humor formally into their agenda, self-advocates and allies disrupt cultural assumptions of intellectual disability as pitiful, repulsive, or childlike. Humor enables nondisabled and disabled people to move through their anxiety, and it is one of the many skills that people with disabilities learn "in order to put the other at their ease."[24]

Disability studies scholars note that humor has a "double-edged nature" for people with disabilities, "constituting them as laughable spectacles in some circumstances and as empowered agents of humor in others."[25] This difference often hinges on who controls, deploys, and sanctions humor in order to create insiders and outsiders.[26] Humor thus reveals and crafts lines of authority and marginalization.[27] Like alliance, however, humor can enforce compulsory capacity. Indeed, people with disabilities serve as a common humorous trope of the "'comic misadventurer,' whose impairments initiate physical comedy or whose body becomes the target for comic violence."[28] In this way, humor marks and ridicules those who disregard or fail to attain compulsory capacity. Humor may be especially difficult to reclaim, as intellectual disabilities make it more difficult to determine who owns and controls humor.[29] Humor can thus work against democratic alliance if we use it to narrow the range of people to whom we make it accessible.

But there are democratic reasons why we would want humor to close off boundaries, especially as a way to create a private space wherein groups that are under siege can seek cover, regroup, and reemerge strengthened. At the SABE conference, Chester Finn often relied on humor. "Why did the self-advocates come to the dinner?" Chester began one evening's events with a joke. "To stuff their faces!" Chester and the crowd laughed. His opening joke says a lot about his humor: he often makes jokes—some funny, some goofy, and a few downright confusing. Upon stepping down from the presidency, he thanked the crowd. "I would just like to thank everyone out there; I enjoyed every minute of it, the names I was called, the threats I received, but it was worth it." In one of the breakout sessions, Jim, a self-advocate leading the session, invited the audience of professionals to consider why self-advocates were so vital to include in deliberation. One professional spoke up: "I'm not in their shoes, so it would be nice to have someone in their shoes to have their own perspective." "So you're saying every shoe is different," Jim said, seeming to weigh her suggestion in a serious tone before he shot back, "Hey, this ain't no booty call!"

These examples show the humorous side of self-advocacy, but they also testify to the ways in which self-advocates use humor purposefully, to destabilize ableist assumptions. When Chester helped orchestrate a vote for a state delegation, Vicki counted the hands raised for each candidate. But she failed to look behind her and thus miscounted the vote. When we realized what happened, the vote was repeated, which was difficult because the three candidates had to maneuver their power wheelchairs in and out of the crowded room. When the candidates were leaving for the second time, Chester said, "I just want to point out that it wasn't me who didn't see all the hands." Chester's humor relieves tensions between abled and nondisabled participants, but unlike Shakespeare's description—which relies on disabled people laughing at their own impairments to relieve anxiety—Chester's humor highlights the flaws of the able-bodied. Chester's sense of humor conveyed more than just an easy laugh, as it destabilized the seeming faultlessness of compulsory capacity.

Self-advocates also used humor to reveal entrenched paternalism. For example, at another panel at SABE, a self-advocate wore a referee outfit, complete with striped shirt, white hat, and whistle. He described the condescending tone and slow speech that nondisabled allies sometimes adopt when talking to him. His strategy: the slower they talk, the slower he responds. We laughed at his mocking slow tone. He also described the "accommodations" that abled advisers offered: "You get extra time to say stuff—what are we auctioneers? . . . But then people start acting professional: there they go with the fancy words again and they begin to hurry things up." He used humor to point out that allies who are committed to inclusion may find that they undermine their own efforts by falling back on habits of efficiency and control.

Similarly, Chester and a team of self-advocates performed a skit at dinner one evening in which Chester played a judge trying to determine if a person working at a sheltered workshop had achieved sufficient skills to obtain competitive employment. "We're here to determine Brian's future," Chester said, and the crowd laughed, already catching the preposterousness of a set of professionals determining someone else's future. "Brian, do you have anything to say?" Chester said, paused fleetingly, and quickly moved on. "Sorry! Out of time! Can anyone else speak for Brian?" The skit conveyed the ways in which professionals can easily outnumber and silence people with intellectual disabilities even in situations in which they are trying to increase a person's level of independence.

By using humor to point out inequality, Chester and other self-advocates navigate tricky territory, as they need to disrupt dominant power hierarchies while maintaining alliances. They invite us to laugh at the ways we perform our anxiety when we practice alliance imperfectly. Humor thus changes the relationship between allies and self-advocates; it upsets the strict power hierarchies of the domination capacity contract, which accords more power to the more abled. In Macpherson's analysis of visually impaired walking groups, she noted how people with disabilities use humor and laughter to negotiate relationships with able-bodied people.[30] Amid these fumbling mistakes, humor can let us practice forgiveness, which Price states is essential to alliance, and which Hannah Arendt argues is essential for action.[31] As we laugh at ourselves and at each other, humor encapsulates our mistakes with grace—under the condition that we can use our laughter to inform our next attempt to practice alliance.

Finally, humor invites and welcomes the unexpected, which often accompanied the self-advocacy gatherings I observed. For example, at a dinner event at SABE, nondisabled speakers commemorated the life of Eunice Kennedy Shriver and her creation and promotion of the Special Olympics. One speaker used much of his time to show video clips of Shriver, one of which was an interview with NBC's Brian Williams. At first, the commemoration of Shriver recalled other keynote panels that I had attended: nondisabled professionals orchestrate the proceedings and invite people with intellectual disabilities to discuss their first-hand experience but then quickly sweep them off the stage. Events took a sharp turn at SABE's dinner, however, when a woman overtook the stage to collect her lost purse. After acquiring the purse, she grabbed the microphone from the nondisabled speaker. "I just want to say a few words," she said, an emotional tone saturating her words. I braced for a story about the Special Olympics. "None of this would be possible without Brian. Without Brian and without NBC, we couldn't have heard Eunice. So watch Brian every night, 6:30 eastern time, on your local NBC affiliate channel." And she marched off the stage. For a moment, I did not know what to do. "That was great!" laughed the woman next to me, and I joined with the crowd in the unexpected humor.

In this moment, the unexpected was in play, but rather than reacting with anxiety or hostility, abled and nondisabled participants responded with humor. Here, the strange and the absurd are not aberrant and unwanted but seized as a way to further disrupt norms of compulsory capacity. Humor, like alliance, is not a principle of personhood; rather, it exposes the ways in which cognitive competence fails to encompass the full range of political tools available to oppressed groups. For Locke, we exercise freedom when our thoughts conform to our actions. According to Arendt, this is Western philosophy's traditional account of freedom-as-sovereignty, which yokes freedom to fantasies of control.[32] But under the purview of SABE's humor, we inhabit an alternative kind of freedom by embracing the unexpected. This is an Arendtian freedom—a willingness to "begin something new and of not being able to control or even foretell its consequences."[33]

Anxiety haunts both sides of humor—both in the ways it can devalue people and the ways it reveals our vulnerability. Self-advocates and allies use humor in multiple ways: to reveal compulsory capacity; to invite the unexpected; to laugh at our fears; and to use this laughter as a way to bind us together, even amid our mistakes.

Dance: Countering Anxiety

Dancing is another tool within the capacity contract that can disrupt our anxiety. Disability scholars have analyzed the role of disabled dance performers to argue that dance is "both an expression of societal values and . . . a vehicle for social change,"[34] noting the ways that disabled dancing bodies challenge norms of embodiment and comportment. When disability studies scholars take up the topic of dance, they often highlight how people with physical disabilities self-consciously use their bodies to challenge performative norms.[35] This positioning reveals differences between disabled performers and an ableist audience. In addition, when scholars take up the performing arts with people with intellectual disabilities, alliance is central, as dance is co-constructed between people.[36]

Like humor and alliance, dance can comply with the domination capacity contract. Dance can normalize our behavior, as the systems that surround it control what constitutes attractive bodies and graceful moves. Nondisabled people may exploit people with intellectual disabilities by using their presence as a "kind of voyeurism . . . with connotations of a freak show."[37] In Nash's study on the emancipatory potential of dance for people with intellectual disabilities, she attempted to get support staff to dance, as a way to eliminate norms of competency in dance. But the staff members more often than not watched, choosing to be audience members rather than participants. Instead of dismantling barriers between abled and disabled, to break hierarchies between staff and clients, Nash's study shows the ways in which dance can operate as a normalizing capacity contract.

For members and allies of SABE, dance is a way of moving in the world detached from compulsory capacity. Movement is a form of communication that people with and without disabilities can access together.[38] Dance offers us a way to contract together in a noncognitive way—to practice alliance in movement. It is a way to celebrate our bodily and mental differences; however, we need to be careful that in celebrating disability as a difference, we do not unwittingly fall back onto "super-crip" narratives, in which empowerment is doing all the things that able-bodied people can do—except better.

Dancing was of central importance during the evening at the Fellowship Group and the SABE conference. At the conference, every night ended with a dance. Following a day of speeches and panels, hotel staff moved tables to the sides of the room in order to open up the middle of the floor for dancing and celebrating. People in wheelchairs; women wearing helmets, dancing alone and together; disabled and nondisabled blurred together: SABE's nightly dance broke out of the traditional confines of political activity. Other disability scholars accord similar levels of importance to dancing—describing the ways people dance or including photographs of people dancing, whether in wheelchairs or with prosthetic or absent limbs—but they have not theorized it as an aspect of disability politics.[39] It is not accidental that disability scholars gravitate toward expressions of dance in their scholarship. Dance accomplishes important tasks for disability rights activists: it reveals the contractual model of personhood and freedom as incomplete, it models alternative modes of connection between persons detached from cognitive competence, and it expresses an enjoyment of life often assumed impossible for people with disabilities. Sami Schalk reflects on the importance of dance at the conference of the Society for Disability Studies, describing its atmosphere as an "ethos of community and love."[40]

Dancing expresses a kind of freedom not well encapsulated by the Lockean and Rawlsian cognitive models. Like speech, it is a form of expression. And, like speech, it can be performed alone, with others, or before an audience. Speech takes on a new and more powerful dimension if done before an audience, and so too is the case with dance. Dancing is also possible with minimal levels of cognition. Before speech can regulate norms of connection, caregivers sway and rock infants to sleep, performing a slow and gentle dance to soothe and comfort tiny babies. Dance is a form of embodied connection in which speech is unnecessary.

Recalling Locke, his conception of autonomy and personal freedom was strongly attached to norms of rationality and the ability of a person to check his actions by his thoughts; in this way, freedom is expressed by the ability to have all actions conform to one's rational preferences and desires.[41] For Locke, impulse negates freedom. By incorporating dance as a pivotal aspect of political mobilization, People First and SABE reveal that the model of freedom and personhood embedded within the normalizing capacity contract is merely a shadow of the full range of expressive actions and modes of connection possible. Although not articulated, People First's and SABE's embrace of dance is a clear critique of the social contract person as not only deficient but also dull.

Dancing is also important for disability rights activists because it embodies an expression of a life well lived, therefore challenging assumptions about the misery and desperation of disabled lives. Although self-advocates and allies can and often do express in words the claim that disabled lives are worthwhile, dancing accomplishes a level of convincing that words by themselves cannot. Like the other tools of humor and alliance, dancing neither articulates a strategy for inclusion nor grounds the essence of personhood. It is instead a tool of disruption—a momentary suspension of norms and a critique of compulsory capacity.

Although we can dance in private or public, dance's public dimension shares in the solidarity capacity contract as something that brings people together. Whether witnessing each other's movements or allowing our bodies to touch and move together, dance is an embodied practice of alliance. Like humor, that can reveal to ourselves our limited natures, so too can dance serve to remind us that how we look and how we move is not the old Lockean model of freedom that looks like mind and body conformity. Instead, freedom is in doing something new, unexpected. It is an Arendtian freedom—spontaneously bringing something forth that cannot last.

Conclusion: Contracting Together

Dance, humor, and alliance reveal to us both ableist anxiety and ways in which we can move within and, at times, beyond anxiety. These tools remind us of the many ways in which we can contract *together*. True, a dominant mode of contracting is through speech, agreement, and consent, but to *contract* is many things: "To enter into, bring upon oneself (involuntarily), incur, catch, acquire, become infected with (something noxious, as disease, mischief; bad habits or condition; danger, risk, blame, guilt)."[42] We can enter into contracts, acquire disabilities, and become infected with anxiety. SABE shows us that we can acquire anxiety and work within it to challenge the meaning of disability. Importantly, SABE shows us that we can contract across profound differences in cognitive capacity—that we can enter into contracts of nondomination even as our anxiety tells us we cannot.

Dance, humor, and alliance return me not only to these sites of activism but also to my relationship with my brother—a fact that took me a long time to realize. Dance returns me to my childhood with my brother, as we often danced together, especially when my parents and sisters left for an evening out. I would blast the radio, and we would dance in our living room. We jumped on the couches and onto tables. My brother would strip off his clothes, and we would wrap ourselves in sheets—our majestic wardrobe. With my brother's autism comes a suspension of norms, and our dance exposed this embodied revelry made possible without judgment. Dance also aptly captures the way my brother moves in the world when he is joyful, as he skips sidewise, leaping and skipping, and then twirls in the air.

Laughing is the surest sign that I know my brother still exists behind the medicinal wall where he now lives. When I visit and he never laughs, I leave feeling empty and unsure of whether he really noticed that I was there. Without the ability to rely on conversation to knit us together, laughter connects us. We laugh as we listen to the car radio blare out the Beach Boys' version of *California Dreamin'* over and over again. When he holds out his arms for a tickle, or his back for me to rub as he laughs, I feel connected. Laughter suspends my anxiety (*Do I visit enough? Does he resent my absence? Is he well taken care of?*) and brings forth his familiar voice. Like other families growing up with children with disabilities, we learned to transform stories of exasperation, shame, and hurt into wild tales of laughter that we retold, embellished, and savored.[43]

Alliance encapsulates a broad and sometimes surprising network of people who help me connect with my brother. For instance, having finished my dissertation, I celebrated a great Christmas with my brother: along with my father and younger sister, we went to KFC for lunch—the first time I had sat down with my father and brother since my brother moved out of our family home. The cashier at KFC had become my father's ally, as she always knew to give my brother a cup for his soda on his entrance into KFC. Even when he snuck into her manager's office to steal her can of Mountain Dew, she laughed instead of yelled. Her acceptance of my brother meant so much to my father that, after lunch, he had me take a picture of both himself and the cashier with their arms around my brother. My father promised that he would send the picture to every manager of KFC to boast of her warmth and patience. Unexpected alliances mean so much when so many reactions are hostile or alarmed.

Going out in public with my brother is risky. Inevitably, if I take him into a store, he manages to run out wildly, usually with stolen cans or bottles of caffeinated soda—a banned substance in his new institutional home. Humor and alliance are tools that we rely on to endure these risks. We look for alliances with strangers—cashiers, restaurant patrons, bystanders—who can respond with humor and not anxiety. We seek out alliances with his paid attendants; I know he has someone special if they laugh with us. When going public fails to go well, we recover by making the misadventure into a new yarn, laughing about the door he tore off the frame, the pants he took off in public, or the food he stole from the strangers at KFC.

If alliance, humor, and dance give us new ways to see the self-advocacy movement, and even new ways for us to reflect on our personal relationships across deep differences in cognitive capacity, what do these tools tell us as political theorists and scholars interested in social contract theory or disability studies? They tell us that capacity contracts are seductive, inevitable, and—occasionally—democratic.

Perhaps you think that the political tools of practicing alliance, humor, and dance are ill equipped to dismantle the normalizing force of the capacity contract. Perhaps they seem flimsy tools on which to demand the full inclusion of people with intellectual disabilities. Indeed, the number of self-advocacy organizations is in decline; funding remains insecure; and prominent self-advocacy leaders are aging, leaving some worried about the movement's future.[44] Amid this precarious existence, isn't the task all that more difficult because these tools—alliance, humor, and dance—always invite normalization?

In fact, I would agree with you. But I would argue that this is the nature of politics, that to look for coherence, closure, and control is to maintain the fictions of the domination capacity contract. These are the same values that penalize people with intellectual disabilities for being incoherent and out of control. Politics is risky. The emancipatory tools we rely on are likely to turn against us. If the normalizing capacity contract gives us anxiety, the democratic capacity contract lets us respond with a conviction of ambivalence. The first sees uncertainty and tries to hide it; the second only sees uncertainty.

But there is a way in which the funkiness and uncertainty of politics is what invites us in. Not the regimen, not the protocol of order and hierarchy, but the laughter, dance, and play of it all. Brooke Ackerly describes the "tyranny of the meeting" as one of the main faults of deliberative democratic theory, as it normalizes social behavior and excludes people who lack the time to attend meetings.[45] The politics of People First and SABE fights against the tyranny of the meeting in that they invite people with a wide range of capacities to participate and, equally important, strive to make politics fun. We act politically by sharing a meal—when doing so makes others uncomfortable or challenges who is deemed fit for public space. We act politically when we throw our bodies in dance—when dominant norms insist that our bodies are best hidden or put out of their misery. We act politically when we open our classrooms to students with intellectual disabilities—as we find ways to practice alliance in academia.

SABE makes us see the stakes of these political actions. At the 2010 national conference's evening ceremony, Chester recognized Nancy Ward for her work as a self-advocate for over twenty years, including being a founding member of SABE and SABE's first chair. On acceptance of her award, Nancy told the audience, "I was hoping that people would be able to dream and those dreams could come true." She then asked the crowd how their lives had changed over the last twenty years: "How many of you live in the community? How many of you have jobs and get this?" Nancy held up her hand and rubbed her fingers together to symbolize cash, and the crowd laughed. "How many of you have friends who aren't paid staff? How many of you have a boyfriend or a girlfriend?" The crowd answered with cheers and applause.

But then Nancy's tone changed, growing louder and more demanding, which in my field notes I tried to capture: "CLOSE DOWN INSTITUTIONS AND HAVE PEOPLE BE A PART OF THEIR COMMUNITIES." The crowd cheered, and Nancy continued in her vision: "CLOSE ALL SHELTERED WORKSHOPS AND HAVE PEOPLE HAVE REAL JOBS AND MAKE REAL MONEY." Amid the applause, a man declared, "This is a revolution!" Nancy has been part of this revolution since 1979, advocating for people to live in their own homes, to live in their own communities, to work, to have friends, and to have sexual partners.

Nancy's call to close institutions and sheltered workshops is a powerful reminder of the ways in which societal and political norms fracture the self-advocacy movement, as many people lack the ability to form new alliances. The contract as a reasoning device sees nothing wrong with the absence of people who cannot reason, but SABE tells us to see it as an injustice. Insofar as we have not created communities in which all people can be a part, then the promise of the emancipatory capacity contract remains unfulfilled. Until then, Nancy and other members of the self-advocacy movement will continue on with the revolution, fighting for people to dream and for those dreams to come true.

Acknowledgments

The idea of this book began to take shape on a warm spring day, courtesy of an ice cream cone and good conversation provided by Alyssa Bernstein. Brooke Ackerly then helped me hone that idea into an argument. More importantly, she taught me that I would need many mentors to help me through graduate school, the writing process, and beyond. There are many different kinds of mentors—coach, critic, friend, cheerleader—and I have had the privilege of finding a lot of them. Here are just a few.

This book would not have been possible without the warm welcome and intellectual curiosity of the many self-advocates with disabilities whom I have met over the years. They have graciously invited me to workshops and conferences, and they have spent extra time answering my questions about the movement.

At Ohio University, I would like to thank Alyssa Bernstein, Susan Burgess, Judith Grant, Ron Hunt, Julie White, and other faculty members and students in the Department of Political Science. Thanks to Vanderbilt University for a graduate fellowship, as well as Vanessa Beasley, James Booth, Joy Calico, Laura Carpenter, Monica Casper, Vera Chatman, Marilyn Friedman, John Geer, Craig Anne Heflinger, Marc Hetherington, Gbemende Johnson, Katie King, Elise McMillan, Emily Nacol, Susan Saegert, Melissa Snarr, and C. Neal Tate. I owe a special thanks to Mona Frederick and the Robert Penn Warren Center for the Humanities at Vanderbilt University for a dissertation fellowship and for hosting a Disability Studies Reading Group. I was also a recipient of a LEND fellowship at Vanderbilt University, which funded some of the fieldwork.

I had the opportunity to present the introduction of this manuscript at the Feminist Pre-conference at the Western Political Science Association. Deep thanks to Joan Tronto, Julie White, Kennan Ferguson, and the audience for offering valuable feedback. Thanks also to Nancy

Hirschmann, Barbara Arneil, and Kristin Bumiller, who have read parts of this manuscript. Brooke Ackerly and Katie King organized a mini-conference at Vanderbilt University for me to share this manuscript with a group of supportive readers. Cricket Keating read the entire manuscript and offered essential feedback and warm support.

I have had the fortune of completing this manuscript on a postdoc-toral research fellowship co-located at Michigan State University and the National University of Ireland in Galway. Thanks to June Chen, Ian Gray, Sister Hegarty, John Kosciulek, Geraldine Leader, Mike Leahy, Josh Plavik, Carolyn Shivers, and Connie Sung. Pieter Martin at the University of Minnesota Press showed early enthusiasm for the project and throughout the process.

I want to thank my parents, Doug and Peggy Clifford, for teaching me most about humor and alliance. My sisters, Beth and Kris, and my brother Matt have inspired much of this project. I'd like to thank the Simplicans for making me part of their family for this entire process. My final thanks goes to Rudy Simplican. He has traveled many places to help see this book finished. Thank you.

Notes

Introduction

1. A pseudonym.

2. In interviews with people with disabilities, Colin Cameron describes how disability is produced in transactions between disabled and nondisabled people when the latter make the former feel uncomfortable and conscious of impairments, such as speech impediments. "Developing an Affirmative Model of Disability and Impairment," in *Disabling Barriers—Enabling Environments,* ed. John Swain, Sally French, Colin Barnes, and Carol Thomas (London: Sage, 2014), 24–30.

3. Ian Hacking cites a common slogan in the autism community that "if you know one person with autism, you know *one* person with autism." "How We Have Been Learning to Talk about Autism: A Role for Stories," *Metaphilosophy* 40, no. 3–4 (2009): 499–516, 503.

4. Rosemarie Garland-Thomson, *Extraordinary Bodies: Figuring Physical Disability in American Culture and Literature* (New York: Columbia University Press, 1997); Dan Goodley, "Jacques Lacan + Paul Hunt = Psychoanalytic Disability Studies," in *Disability and Social Theory: New Developments and Directions,* ed. Dan Goodley, Bill Hughes, and Lennard Davis (New York: Palgrave Macmillan, 2012), 179–94.

5. Fiona Kumari Campbell, "Stalking Ableism: Using Disability to Expose 'Abled' Narcissism," in *Disability and Social Theory: New Developments and Directions,* ed. Dan Goodley, Bill Hughes, and Lennard Davis (New York: Palgrave Macmillan, 2012), 212–30; Bill Hughes, "Civilizing Modernity and the Ontological Invalidation of Disabled People," in *Disability and Social Theory: New Developments and Directions,* ed. Dan Goodley, Bill Hughes, and Lennard Davis (New York: Palgrave Macmillan, 2012), 17–32; Margrit Shildrick, *Dangerous Discourses of Disability, Subjectivity and Sexuality* (New York: Palgrave Macmillan, 2009); Margrit Shildrick, "Dangerous Discourses: Anxiety, Desire, and Disability," *Studies in Gender and Sexuality* 8, no. 3 (2007): 221–44; Harlan Hahn, "The Politics of Physical Difference: Disability and Discrimination," *Journal of Social Issues* 44, no. 1 (1988): 39–47.

6. Carrie Sandahl and Philip Auslander, eds., *Bodies in Commotion: Disability and Performance* (Ann Arbor: University of Michigan Press, 2005).

7. Hahn, "The Politics of Physical Difference," 42.

8. Ibid., 43.

9. Shakespeare, *Macbeth*, act 5, scene 5.

10. Rosemarie Garland-Thomson, *Staring: How We Look* (Oxford: Oxford University Press, 2009), 10.

11. Ibid., 38; emphasis added. In addition, Lennard Davis analyzes the concept of obsession—noting that the concept can refer to a specific medical diagnosis as well as a cultural trait that applies to people's behavior broadly. See *Obsession: A History* (Chicago: University of Chicago Press, 2008).

12. Jackie Leach Scully, *Disability Bioethics: Moral Bodies, Moral Difference* (Lanham, Md.: Rowman & Littlefield, 2008). See also Paul Hunt, "A Critical Condition," in *Stigma: The Experience of Disability*, ed. Paul Hunt (London: Geoffrey Chapman, 1966).

13. Brien A. Nosek, Frederick L. Smyth, Jeffrey J. Hansen, Thierry Devos, Nicole M. Lindner, Kate A. Ranganath, Colin Tucker Smith, Kristina R. Olson, Dolly Chuch, Anthony G. Greenwald, and Mahzarin R. Banaji, "Pervasiveness and Correlates of Implicit Attitudes and Stereotypes," *European Review of Social Psychology* 18, no. 1 (2007): 1–53, 18–19.

14. Shaun Grech, "Disability and the Majority World: A Neocolonial Approach," in *Disability and Social Theory: New Developments and Directions*, ed. Dan Goodley, Bill Hughes, and Lennard Davis (New York: Palgrave Macmillan, 2012), 52–69.

15. Campbell, "Stalking Ableism"; David Serlin, *Replaceable You: Engineering the Body in Postwar America* (Chicago: University of Chicago Press, 2004).

16. Carole Pateman, *The Sexual Contract* (Stanford: Stanford University Press, 1988); Charles W. Mills, *The Racial Contract* (Ithaca, N.Y.: Cornell University Press, 1997).

17. Those who assume that surrogates should represent people with profound forms of cognitive impairments include Martha Nussbaum, "The Capabilities of People with Cognitive Disabilities," *Metaphilosophy* 40, no. 3–4 (2009): 331–51; Michael Bérubé, "Equality, Freedom, and/or Justice for All: A Response to Martha Nussbaum," *Metaphilosophy* 40, no. 3–4 (2009): 352–65; Licia Carlson, "Who's the Expert? Rethinking Authority in the Face of Intellectual Disability," *Journal of Intellectual Disability Research* 54, no. 1 (2009): 58–65.

18. John Rawls, *Political Liberalism* (New York: Columbia University Press, 2005); Eva Feder Kittay, *Love's Labor: Essays on Women, Equality, and Dependency* (New York: Routledge, 1999). For a review of these debates, see the special issue on disability in *Metaphilosophy* 40, no. 3–4 (2009), and the ed-

ited volume that came out of that issue: Eva Feder Kittay and Licia Carlson, *Cognitive Disability and Its Challenge to Moral Philosophy* (Oxford: Wiley-Blackwell, 2010).

19. Shildrick, "Dangerous Discourses."

20. Jenny Morris, "Impairment and Disability: Constructing an Ethics of Care That Promotes Human Rights," *Hypatia* 16, no. 4 (2001): 1–16.

21. This task follows from Michel Foucault's concept of problematization and the need to reproblematize concepts to reveal new possibilities for freedom, a discussion of which can be found in *The Essential Foucault: Selections from the Essential Works of Foucault, 1954–1984*, ed. Paul Rabinow and Nikolas Rose (New York: New Press, 2003).

22. Kim Nielsen, *A Disability History of the United States* (Boston: Beacon Press, 2012).

23. According to Nussbaum, voting and serving on a jury are two of the most pressing political problems facing people with intellectual disabilities. Nussbaum, "The Capabilities of People with Cognitive Disabilities."

24. The approaches of Jeff McMahan and Peter Singer are both prominent and troubling in this regard. For examples, see Jeff McMahan, "Cognitive Disability and Cognitive Enhancement," *Metaphilosophy* 40, no. 3–4 (2009): 582–605; Peter Singer, "Ethics and Disability: A Response to Koch," *Journal of Disability Policy Studies* 16, no. 2 (2005): 130–33.

25. Campbell, "Stalking Ableism," 212.

26. Simi Linton, *My Body Politic: A Memoir* (Ann Arbor: University of Michigan Press, 2007); James I. Charlton, *Nothing about Us without Us: Disability Oppression and Empowerment* (Berkeley: University of California Press, 1998); Tom Shakespeare, "The Social Model of Disability," in *The Disability Studies Reader,* 2nd ed., ed. Lennard J. Davis (New York: Routledge, 2006), 197–204.

27. Sandahl and Auslinger, *Bodies in Commotion,* 129; Christopher Donoghue, "Challenging the Authority of the Medical Definition of Disability: An Analysis of the Resistance to the Social Constructionist Paradigm," *Disability & Society* 18, no. 2 (2003): 199–208.

28. Kristin Bumiller, "The Geneticization of Autism: From New Reproductive Technologies to the Conception of Genetic Normalcy," *Signs* 34, no. 4 (Summer 2009): 875–99.

29. "Frequently Asked Questions on Intellectual Disability," www.aaidd.org.

30. C. F. Goodey, "What Is Developmental Disability? The Origin and Nature of Our Conceptual Models," *Journal on Developmental Disabilities* 8, no. 2 (2009): 1–18.

31. Henry H. Goddard, "Who Is a Moron?," *Scientific Monthly* 24, no. 1 (1927): 41–46.

32. For instance, a woman with asymptomatic HIV was considered disabled due to her inability to raise and bear children (*Bragden v. Abbott*, 524 U.S. 624 [1998]), but a man with mental retardation was ruled not disabled enough because it "is unclear whether thinking, communicating and social interaction are 'major life activities' under the ADA" (*Littleton v. Wal-Mart Stores, Inc.*, 231 Fed. Appx. 874 [11th Cir. 2007]).

33. Constitutional or statutory enfranchisement restrictions affecting people with disabilities exist in forty-one states. See Daniel P. Tokaji and Ruth Colker, "Absentee Voting by People with Disabilities: Promoting Access and Integrity," *McGeorge Law Review* 38 (2007): 1015–64, 1028. See also Pamela S. Karlan, "Framing the Voting Rights Claims of Cognitively Impaired Individuals," *McGeorge Law Review* 38 (2007): 917–30.

34. On legal matters, see Christopher Slobogin, *Minding Justice: Laws That Deprive People with Mental Disability of Life and Liberty* (Cambridge, Mass.: Harvard University Press, 2006).

35. Theo Blackmore and Stephen Lee Hodgkins, "Discourses and Disabled Peoples' Organizations: Foucault, Bourdieu and Future Perspectives," in *Disability and Social Theory: New Developments and Directions*, ed. Dan Goodley, Bill Hughes, and Lennard Davis (New York: Palgrave Macmillan, 2012), 70–87.

36. For estimated rates of abortions related to Down syndrome, see Amy Harmon, "Prenatal Test Puts Down Syndrome in Hard Focus," *New York Times*, May 9, 2007. See also Caroline Mansfield, Suellen Hopfer, and Theresa M. Marteau, "Termination Rates after Prenatal Diagnosis of Down Syndrome, Spina Bifida, Anencephaly, and Turner and Klinefelter Syndromes: A Systematic Literature Review," *Prenatal Diagnosis* 19, no. 9 (1999): 808–12. In comparison, analysts of sex-selective abortion in India suggest that "almost 94 percent of the female fetuses of women receiving ultrasound or amniocentesis were *not* aborted." Fred Arnold, Sunita Kishor, and T. K. Roy, "Sex-Selective Abortions in India," *Population and Development Review* 28, no. 4 (2002): 759–85, 778.

37. My analysis of the number of missing people with disabilities is informed by Amartya Sen's similar analysis of missing women; he estimates that social disadvantage accounts for over 100 million missing women across the globe. Amartya Sen, "Missing Women," *British Medical Journal* 304 (March 1992): 587–88, 587.

38. Sharon L. Snyder and David T. Mitchell, *Cultural Locations of Disability* (Chicago: University of Chicago Press, 2006).

39. Licia Carlson, "Who's the Expert?," 58–65; Licia Carlson, "Philosophers of Intellectual Disability: A Taxonomy," *Metaphilosophy* 40, no. 3–4 (2009): 552–66.

40. Robert McRuer, *Crip Theory: Cultural Signs of Queerness and Disability* (New York: New York University Press, 2006); Lennard J. Davis, *Bending over Backwards: Disability, Dismodernism, and Other Difficult Positions* (New York: New York University Press, 2002); Snyder and Mitchell, *Cultural Locations of Disability*.

41. Dorothea L. Dix, *On Behalf of the Insane Poor: Selected Reports* (New York: Arno Press and New York Times, 1971). For excellent histories detailing state policies and practices around people with intellectual disabilities, see Steven Noll, *Feeble-Minded in Our Midst: Institutions for the Mentally Retarded in the South, 1900–1940* (Chapel Hill: University of North Carolina Press, 1995); Steven Noll and James W. Trent, *Mental Retardation in America: A Historical Reader* (New York: New York University Press, 2004); James W. Trent, *Inventing the Feeble Mind: A History of Mental Retardation in the United States* (Berkeley: University of California Press, 1994).

42. Their accounts appeared in local newspapers, *Life* magazine, *Reader's Digest,* and the book *Out of Sight, Out of Mind.* Steven J. Taylor, "Conscientious Objectors of WWII," *Washington Post,* May 28, 2009.

43. On care theory, see Maureen Sander-Staudt, "The Unhappy Marriage of Care Ethics and Virtue Ethics," *Hypatia* 21, no. 4 (2006): 21–39, 36. See also Barbara Arneil, "Disability, Self Image, and Modern Political Thought," *Political Theory* 20, no. 10 (2009): 1–25.

44. Daniel Engster, "Care Ethics and Natural Law Theory: Toward an Institutional Political Theory of Caring," *Journal of Politics* 66, no. 1 (2004): 113–35, 114.

45. Kittay, *Love's Labor,* 65, 162.

46. For Cooper, idealizing tendencies accompany care theory more broadly. Davina Cooper, "'Well, You Go There to Get Off': Visiting Feminist Care Ethics through a Women's Bathhouse," *Feminist Theory* 8 no. 3 (2007): 243–62.

47. Eva Feder Kittay, "Beyond Autonomy and Paternalism: The Caring Transparent Self," in *Autonomy & Paternalism: Reflections on the Theory and Practice of Health Care,* ed. Thomas Nys, Yvonne Denier, and Toon Vandevelde (Belgium: Peeters Publishers, 2007), 23–70, 53.

48. Kittay, *Love's Labor,* 52.

49. Shiloh Whitney, "Dependency Relations: Corporeal Vulnerability and Norms of Personhood in Hobbes and Kittay," *Hypatia* 26, no. 3 (2007): 554–74. Engster has made similar critiques of the early work of Nel Noddings in "Care Ethics and Natural Law Theory." See also Stacy Clifford Simplican, "Care, Disability, and Violence: Theorizing Complex Dependency in Eva Kittay and Judith Butler," *Hypatia* 30, no. 1 (2015).

50. Bill Hughes, Linda McKie, Debra Hopkins, and Nick Watson, "Love's Labors Lost? Feminism, the Disabled People's Movement and an Ethic of Care," *Sociology* 39, no. 2 (2005): 259–75.

51. Kittay, *Love's Labor*, 152.

52. Ibid., 166.

53. As Bérubé points out, these connections between care and affection are dangerous, as many parents of autistic children have gently reminded him. Bérubé, "Equality, Freedom, and/or Justice for All."

54. Martha C. Nussbaum, *Frontiers of Justice: Disability, Nationality, Species Membership* (Cambridge, Mass.: Belknap Press of Harvard University Press, 2006).

55. Michael Bérubé, *Life as We Know it: A Father, a Family, and an Exceptional Child* (New York: Vintage Books, 1998).

56. Roger S. Gottlieb, "The Tasks of Embodied Love: Moral Problems in Caring for Children with Disabilities," *Hypatia* 17, no. 3 (2002): 225–36.

57. Sophia Isako Wong, "At Home with Down Syndrome and Gender," *Hypatia* 17, no. 3 (2002): 89–117.

58. Carolyn Ellis and Arthur P. Bochner, "Telling and Performing Personal Stories: The Constraints of Choice in Abortion," in *Investigating Subjectivity: Research on Lived Experience*, ed. Carolyn Ellis and Michael C. Flaherty (London: Sage Publications, 1992), 79–101. Carolyn Ellis describes autoethnography as if she were speaking to students on the first day of class: "We'll view ourselves as part of the research—sometimes as our focus—rather than standing outside what we do. Instead of starting with hypotheses, we'll emphasize writing as a process of discovery." Ellis, *The Ethnographic I: A Methodological Novel about Ethnography* (Walnut Creek, Calif.: AltaMira Press, 2004), 3.

59. For example, in "Telling and Performing Personal Stories," Ellis and Bochner compose a co-constructed narrative as a therapeutic way to process Ellis's own decision to abort a pregnancy during their relationship.

60. Jen Rinaldi, "Reflexivity in Research: Disability between the Lines," *Disability Studies Quarterly* 33, no. 2 (2013).

61. Ibid.

62. Thomas G. Couser, "The Empire of the 'Normal': A Forum on Disability and Self-Representation: Introduction," *American Quarterly* 52, no. 2 (2000): 305–10, 305.

63. Thomson, "Dares to Stares: Disabled Women Performance Artists & the Dynamics of Staring," in *Bodies in Commotion: Disability and Performance*, ed. Carrie Sandahl and Philip Auslander (Ann Arbor: University of Michigan Press, 2005), 30–41.

64. In 2013, *Disability Studies Quarterly* featured a special issue on reflexivity. See, in particular, Joan M. Ostrove and Jennifer Rinaldi, "Guest Editors' Introduction—Self-Reflection as Scholarly Praxis: Researcher Identity in Disability Studies," *Disability Studies Quarterly* 33, no. 2 (2013), and Corbett Joan

O'Toole, "Disclosing Our Relationships to Disabilities: An Invitation for Disability Studies Scholars," *Disability Studies Quarterly* 33, no. 2 (2013).

65. Licia Carlson, *The Faces of Intellectual Disability: Philosophical Reflections* (Bloomington: Indiana University Press, 2010).

66. Bill Hughes and Kevin Paterson, "The Social Model of Disability and the Disappearing Body: Towards a Sociology of Impairment," *Disability & Society* 12, no. 3 (1997): 325–40; Tobin Siebers, "Disability in Theory: From Social Constructionism to the New Realism of the Body," *American Literary History* 13, no. 4 (2001): 737–54.

67. Couser, "Introduction," 309.

68. David T. Mitchell, "Body Solitaire: The Singular Subject of Disability Autobiography," *American Quarterly* 52, no. 2 (2000): 311–15, 311.

69. Jan Walmsley, "Normalisation, Emancipatory Research and Inclusive Research in Learning Disability," *Disability & Society* 16, no. 2 (2001): 187–205, 194–95.

70. O'Toole, "Disclosing Our Relationships to Disabilities."

71. Daniel Engster, "Rethinking Care Theory: The Practice of Caring and the Obligation to Care," *Hypatia* 20, no. 3 (2005): 50–74, 54; emphasis in the original.

72. Tronto suggests that the first stage of care, attentiveness, is capable of destabilizing perspectives and creating shifts in power. See "Care as a Basis for Radical Political Judgments," *Hypatia* 10, no. 2 (1995): 141–49.

73. Ari Ne'eman voiced these concerns at the 2011 Annual Conference for the American Political Science Association.

74. Judith Butler focuses on people who take up oppositional standpoints, not the disabled, in *Precarious Life: The Powers of Mourning and Violence* (London: Verso, 2004), xix.

75. Lisa Vanhala, *Making Rights a Reality? Disability Rights Activists and Legal Mobilization* (Oxford: Oxford University Press, 2011).

76. O'Toole, "Disclosing Our Relationships to Disabilities."

77. Davis, *Bending over Backwards*, 11.

78. Sandanl and Auslinger, *Bodies in Commotion*, 8.

79. Garland-Thomson, *Extraordinary Bodies*, 6.

80. Tobin Siebers, "Disability and the Theory of Complex Embodiment," in *The Disability Studies Reader*, 4th ed., ed. Lennard Davis (New York: Routledge, 2013), 275–283.

81. On the use of identity in the disability movement, see Susan Peters, Susan Gabel, and Simoni Symeonidou, "Resistance, Transformation and the Politics of Hope: Imagining a Way Forward for the Disabled People's Movement," *Disability & Society* 24, no. 5 (2009): 543–556.

82. Christine Kelly, "Wrestling with Group Identity: Disability Activism and Direct Funding," *Disability Studies Quarterly* 30, no. 3/4 (2010).

83. Davis, *Bending over Backwards*, 5.

84. Brueggemann, "Delivering Disability, Willing Speech," in *Bodies in Commotion: Disability and Performance*, ed. Carrie Sandahl and Philip Auslander (Ann Arbor: University of Michigan Press, 2005), 17–29.

85. Denise Walsh, *Women's Rights in Democratizing States: Just Debate and Gender Justice in the Public Sphere* (Cambridge: Cambridge University Press, 2011).

86. Iris Marion Young, *Inclusion and Democracy* (Oxford: Oxford University Press, 2000).

87. Stacy Clifford, "Making Disability Public in Deliberative Democracy," *Contemporary Political Theory* 11, no. 2 (2012): 211–28.

88. See, for example, Jürgen Habermas, "On Systematically Distorted Communication," *Inquiry* 13, no. 1 (1970): 205–18.

89. For political theory's paradoxical obsession with order, see Adriana Cavarero, "Politicizing Theory," *Political Theory* 30, no. 4 (2002): 506–32.

90. Brueggemann, "Delivering Disability, Willing Speech," 19.

91. Ibid.

92. Research shows that many professionals who work with people with disabilities may have underlying negative perceptions about disability of which they are unaware. Researchers argue that making people aware of their negative perceptions is crucial to fostering new and more positive associations. See Steven R. Pruett and Fong Chan, "The Development and Psychometric Validation of the Disability Attitude Implicit Association Test," *Rehabilitation Psychology* 51, no. 3 (2007): 202–13.

93. Wendy Brown, "At the Edge," *Political Theory* 30, no. 4 (2002): 556–76.

94. Hacking, "How We Have Been Learning to Talk about Autism."

95. Charles W. Mills, "'Ideal Theory' as Ideology," *Hypatia* 20, no. 3 (2005): 165–84.

96. Carol Gilligan's work in psychology is a classic example; see Gilligan, *In a Different Voice: Psychological Theory and Women's Development* (Cambridge, Mass.: Harvard University Press, 1982). Other feminist work that uses empirical work to inform normative theory includes Brooke A. Ackerly, *Universal Human Rights in a World of Difference* (Cambridge: Cambridge University Press, 2008); Brooke A. Ackerly, *Political Theory and Feminist Social Criticism* (Cambridge: Cambridge University Press, 2000); Cristina Beltrán, "Going Public: Hannah Arendt, Immigrant Action, and the Space of Appearance," *Political Theory* 37, no. 5 (2009): 595–622; and Saba Mahmood, *Politics of Piety: The Islamic Revival and the Feminist Subject* (Princeton: Princeton University Press, 2005).

97. Griet Roets and Rosi Braidotti, "Nomadology and Subjectivity: Deleuze, Guattari and Critical Disability Studies," in *Disability and Social Theory: New Developments and Directions*, ed. Dan Goodley, Bill Hughes, and Lennard Davis (New York: Palgrave Macmillan, 2012), 161–78. The inclusion of disabled people, however, is controversial. For Sharon Snyder and David Mitchell, "Beneath the guise of a leftist agenda of disability-centered research, we still reproduce an intense degree of oppression in the name of a newfound respect for disabled people's input into the bottomless well of our quest for disability knowledge." Snyder and Mitchell, *Cultural Locations of Disability*, 199.

98. I also received IRB approval.

99. Simone Aspis, "Self-Advocacy: Vested Interests and Misunderstandings," *British Journal of Learning Disabilities* 30, no. 1 (2002): 3–7.

100. Jo Aldridge, "Picture This: The Use of Participatory Photographic Research Methods with People with Learning Disabilities," *Disability & Society* 22, no. 1 (2007): 1–17.

101. Michael V. Angrosino, *Opportunity House: Ethnographic Stories of Mental Retardation* (Walnut Creek, Calif.: AltaMira Press, 1998).

1. Locke's Capacity Contract and the Construction of Idiocy

1. Chana Joffe-Walt, Unfit for Work: The Startling Rise of Disability in America, NPR, March 29, 2013, http://apps.npr.org/unfit-for-work.

2. Wynton Hall, "Government Spends More on Disability than Food Stamps, Welfare Combined," Brietbart, March 25, 2013, www.breitbart.com /Big-Government/2013/03/25/Govt-Spends-More-On-Disability-Than -Food-Stamps-And-Welfare-Combined.

3. Lennard Davis, "NPR Reporter Chana Joffe-Walt Gets Disability Wrong," *Huffington Post*, March 29, 2013, www.huffingtonpost.com/lennard -davis/npr-reporter-chana-joffew_b_2971443.html.

4. Nancy J. Hirschmann, "Disability as a New Frontier for Feminist Intersectionality Research," *Politics & Gender* 8, no. 3 (2012): 396–405.

5. Rawls, *Political Liberalism*.

6. Nussbaum, *Frontiers of Justice*, 100; Christie Hartley, "Disability and Justice," *Philosophy Compass* 6, no. 2 (2011): 120–32, 120; Licia Carlson and Eva Feder Kittay, "Introduction: Rethinking Philosophical Presumptions in Light of Cognitive Disability," *Metaphilosophy* 40, no. 3–4 (2009): 307–30, 310.

7. Arneil, "Disability, Self Image, and Modern Political Thought," 1–25; Iris Marion Young, "Taking the Basic Structure Seriously," *Perspectives on Politics* 4, no. 1 (2006): 91–97.

8. Uday Sing Mehta, *The Anxiety of Freedom: Imagination and Individuality in Locke's Political Thought* (Ithaca, N.Y.: Cornell University Press, 1992);

Ronald Terchek, *Republican Paradoxes and Liberal Anxieties: Retrieving Neglected Fragments of Political Theory* (Lanham, Md.: Rowman & Littlefield, 1997).

9. John Locke, *The Two Treatises of Government,* ed. Peter Laslett (Cambridge: Cambridge University Press, 2004), 2.4.

10. John Locke, *An Essay Concerning Human Understanding,* ed. Peter H. Nidditch (Oxford: Oxford University Press, 1979).

11. On an overview of disability in Western political thought, see Arneil, "Disability, Self Image, and Modern Political Thought." On the limits of Lockean equality, see Jeremy Waldron, *God, Locke, and Equality: Christian Foundations of John Locke's Political Thought* (Cambridge: Cambridge University Press, 2002). On Aristotelian notions of species, see Michael R. Ayers, "Locke versus Aristotle on Natural Kinds," *Journal of Philosophy* 78, no. 5 (1981): 247–72.

12. C. F. Goodey, *A History of Intelligence and "Intellectual Disability": The Shaping of Psychology in Early Modern Europe* (Farnham, UK: Ashgate, 2013); David Braddock, *Disability at the Dawn of the 21st Century and the State of the States* (Washington D.C.: American Association on Mental Retardation, 2001); C. F. Goodey and Tim Stainton, "Intellectual Disability and the Myth of the Changeling Myth," *Journal of the History of the Behavioral Sciences* 37, no. 3 (Summer 2001): 223–40.

13. Pateman, *The Sexual Contract;* Mills, *The Racial Contract.* On the domination contract, see Charles W. Mills, "The Domination Contract," in *Illusion of Consent: Engaging with Carole Patemen,* ed. Daniel O'Neill, Mary Lyndon Shanley, and Iris Marion Young (University Park: Pennsylvania State University Press, 2008), 49–74.

14. Brooke A. Ackerly, "Human Rights and the Epistemology of Social Contract Theory," in *Illusion of Consent: Engaging with Carole Patemen,* ed. Daniel O'Neill, Mary Lyndon Shanley, and Iris Marion Young (University Park: Pennsylvania State University Press, 2008), 75–95, 77; emphasis in the original.

15. Christine Keating, *Decolonizing Democracy: Transforming the Social Contract in India* (University Park: Pennsylvania State University Press, 2011).

16. Susan Burgess and Christine (Cricket) Keating, "Occupy the Social Contract! Participatory Democracy and Iceland's Crowd-Sourced Constitution," *New Political Science* 35, no. 3 (2013): 417–31.

17. Nancy J. Hirschmann, "Intersectionality before Intersectionality Was Cool: The Importance of Class to Feminist Interpretations of Locke," in *Feminist Interpretations of John Locke,* ed. Nancy J. Hirschmann and Kirstie M. McClure (University Park: Pennsylvania State University Press, 2007), 155–86, 181.

18. William Little, H. W. Fowler, and J. Coulson, *The Shorter Oxford English Dictionary on Historical Principles,* 3rd ed. (Oxford: Clarendon Press, 1973), 952.

19. *Oxford English Dictionary,* www.oed.com.

20. Thomas Hobbes, *Leviathan* (Oxford: Oxford University Press, 1998), 96. Also difficult is that histories of idiocy seldom predate the nineteenth century, in part due to the lack of documentation before the rise of residential institutions. C. F. Goodey, "The Psychopolitics of Learning and Disability in Seventeenth-Century Thought," in *From Idiocy to Mental Deficiency: Historical Perspectives on People with Learning Disabilities,* ed. David Wright and Anne Digby (London: Routledge, 1996), 93–117.

21. Enid Welsford, *The Fool: His Social and Literary History* (New York: Farrar & Rinehart, 1935).

22. Sandra Billington, *A Social History of the Fool* (New York: Harvester Press, 1984), 12.

23. Ibid.

24. Ibid., 33.

25. Richard Neugebauer, "Mental Handicap in Medieval and Early Modern England: Criteria, Measurement and Care," in *From Idiocy to Mental Deficiency: Historical Perspectives on People with Learning Disabilities,* ed. David Wright and Anne Digby (London: Routledge, 1996), 22–43, 26.

26. Ibid.

27. Richard Neugebauer, "Exploitation of the Insane in the New World: Benoni Buck, the First Reported Case of Mental Retardation in the American Colonies," *Archives of General Psychiatry* 44, no. 5 (1987): 481–83.

28. Sir Edward Coke, "Beverley's Case of Non Compos Mentis," in *The Reports of Sir Edward Coke* (London: R. Pheney, 1826), 568–78.

29. D. Christopher Gabbard, "From Idiot Beast to Idiot Sublime: Mental Disability in John Cleland's *Fanny Hill,*" *PMLA* 123 (2008): 375–89.

30. Billington, *Social History of the Fool,* 17.

31. Goodey, "What Is Developmental Disability?," 1–18, 9–10.

32. Sarah R. Cohen, "Chardin's Fur: Painting, Materialism, and the Question of Animal Soul," *Eighteenth-Century Studies* 38, no. 1 (2004): 39–61, 45; emphasis added.

33. Thomas Willis, *Two Discourses Concerning the Soul of Brutes, Which Is That of the Vital and Sensitive of Man* (Gainesville, Fla. Scholars' Facsimiles & Reprints, 1971).

34. Gabbard, "Idiot Beast to Idiot Sublime," 380.

35. John Dunn, *Locke* (Oxford: Oxford University Press, 1984), 30.

36. Editor's introduction to *The Two Treatises of Civil Government,* 84.

37. Waldron, *God, Locke, and Equality,* 103.

38. C. B. MacPherson, *The Political Theory of Possessive Individualism: Hobbes to Locke* (Oxford: Clarendon Press, 1962); Nancy J. Hirschmann and Kirstie M. McClure, eds., *Feminist Interpretations of John Locke* (University Park:

Pennsylvania State University Press, 2007); Mehta, *The Anxiety of Freedom*; Andrew Dilts, "'To Kill a Thief': Punishment, Proportionality, and Criminal Subjectivity in Locke's *Second Treatise*," *Political Theory* 40, no. 1 (2012): 58–83; Rebecca Kingston, "Locke, Waldron and the Moral Status of 'Crooks,'" *European Journal of Political Theory* 7, no. 2 (2008): 203–21.

39. William Uzgalis, *John Locke's Essay Concerning Human Understanding* (New York: Continuum, 2007), 3.

40. Kenneth Dewhurst, *John Locke (1632–1704), Physician and Philosopher* (New York: Garland, 1984).

41. For an analysis of Locke's worldview according to a great chain of being, see Kirstie McClure, *Judging Rights: Lockean Politics and the Limits of Consent* (Ithaca, N.Y.: Cornell University Press, 1996).

42. In-text citations to the *Essay* refer to the book, chapter, and paragraph.

43. John Locke, *Locke: Political Essays*, ed. Mark Goldie (Cambridge: Cambridge University Press, 1997), 85. See also *Essay*, 2.2.4.

44. My understanding of the idiot's epistemological role builds on Andrew Dilts's analysis of the thief in Locke's *Treatise*; see Dilts, "'To Kill a Thief.'"

45. In the seventeenth century, "drills" referred to a West African species of baboon. See *Oxford English Dictionary*, www.oed.com.

46. Locke, *Locke*, 99.

47. Ibid., 113n.34.

48. On the link and risks between madness and passion, see Mehta, *The Anxiety of Freedom*.

49. *Oxford English Dictionary*, www.oed.com.

50. John W. Yolton, *A Locke Dictionary* (Oxford: Blackwell, 1993), 36; Christopher Hughes Conn, *Locke on Essence and Identity* (Boston: Kluwer Academic Publishers, 2003), 44; Anthony Krupp, *Reason's Children: Childhood in Early Modern Philosophy* (Lewisburg, Penn.: Bucknell University Press, 2009), 80.

51. Goodey and Stainton, "Intellectual Disability and the Myth of the Changeling Myth."

52. C. F. Goodey, "John Locke's Idiots in the Natural History of Mind," *History of Psychiatry* 5 (1994): 215–50, 215.

53. See also Ayers, "Locke versus Aristotle on Natural Kinds," 259n.12.

54. Locke, *Second Treatise*, 2.14.

55. Locke, *Second Treatise*, 13.157; see also 21.224; Emily Nacol, "The Risks of Political Authority: Trust, Knowledge and Political Agency in Locke's Second Treatise," *Political Studies* 59 (2001): 580–95.

56. Locke, *An Essay Concerning Human Understanding*, 344.

57. It may seem appropriate to look for solutions in *Some Thoughts on Education*, as Locke outlines how to avoid the miscarriages of reason that the *Essay*

documents, but his education advice is problematic. First, Locke targets his educational reform at the sons of gentlemen only, and the individualized instruction makes it impossible to universalize. See Luigi Bradizza, "Elite Education and the Viability of a Lockean Society," *Review of Politics* 70, no. 4 (2008): 547–71. Scholars also raise problems concerning the ways in which Locke's educational regimen requires fathers to indoctrinate their sons into the love of reason based on internal desires for recognition. See Ruth Grant, "John Locke on Custom's Power and Reason's Authority," *Review of Politics* 74, no. 4 (2012): 607–29; James Tully, "Governing Conduct: Locke on the Reform of Thought and Behavior," in *An Approach to Political Philosophy: Locke in Contexts*, ed. Quentin Skinner (Cambridge: Cambridge University Press, 1993), 179–241.

58. Locke, *Second Treatise*, 2.4.

59. Ibid., 2.6.

60. Ibid., 6.60.

61. Kathy Squadrito, "Locke and the Dispossession of the American Indian," in *Philosophers on Race: Critical Essays*, ed. Julie K. Ward and Tommy L. Lott (Oxford: Blackwell, 2002), 145–81.

62. On Locke's grant of charity, see Arneil, "Disability, Self Image, and Modern Political Thought," 222.

63. Waldron, *God, Locke, and Equality*.

64. Douglas John Casson, *Liberating Judgment: Fanatics, Skeptics, and John Locke's Politics and Probability* (Princeton: Princeton University Press, 2011); Steven Forde, "What Does Locke Expect Us to Know?," *Review of Politics* 68, no. 2 (2006): 232–58; Grant, "John Locke on Custom's Power."

65. Mark E. Button, *Contract, Culture, and Citizenship: Transformative Liberalism from Hobbes to Rawls* (University Park: Pennsylvania State University Press, 2008), 89.

66. Carole Pateman, "Race, Sex, and Indifference," in *Contract and Domination*, ed. Carole Pateman and Charles Mills (Cambridge: Polity, 2007), 134–64, 137.

67. Dilts, "'To Kill a Thief.'"

68. Locke, *Second Treatise*, 16.176.

69. Ibid., 8.98.

70. Ibid., 21.223.

71. Ibid., 21.225.

72. Ibid.

73. Joan Tronto, *Caring Democracy: Markets, Equality, and Justice* (New York: New York University Press, 2013), 10.

74. Waldron, *God, Locke, and Equality*, 80; emphasis in the original.

75. Mills, "The Domination Contract."

76. Robert McRuer, *Crip Theory: Cultural Signs of Queerness and Disability* (New York: New York University Press, 2006). Amber Knight, however, takes

a similar example of building solidarity through uncertainty and argues that it fails to move disability rights activism forward in meaningful ways. "Disability as Vulnerability: Redistributing Precariousness in Democratic Ways," *Journal of Politics* 76, no. 1 (January 2014): 15–26.

77. A. S. Kanter, "The Promise and Challenge of the United Nations Convention on the Rights of Persons with Disabilities," *Syracuse Journal of International Law and Commerce* 34 (2006): 287–321.

2. Manufacturing Anxiety

1. Emilie Dionne, "Book Review: Dangerous Discourses of Disability, Subjectivity, and Sexuality," *Hypatia* 26, no. 3 (Summer 2011): 659; emphasis in the original.

2. Hunt, "A Critical Condition."

3. Hirschmann, "Disability as a New Frontier for Feminist Intersectionality Research," 396–405, 400. Amber Knight gives the same example of the threat of becoming disabled. See "Disability as Vulnerability: Redistributing Precariousness in Democratic Ways," *Journal of Politics* 76, no. 1 (January 2014): 15–26.

4. McRuer, *Crip Theory*, 197.

5. Hirschmann, "Disability as a New Frontier," 400.

6. As Elizabeth Ettorre describes, "if we refuse to accept modernist notions of an unchanging natural body and a total self identity marked by this body, we help to create an 'ethical moment.'" Ettorre, "Review Article: Reshaping the Space between Bodies and Culture: Embodying the Biomedicalized Body," *Sociology of Health & Illness* 20, no. 4 (July 1998): 548–55, 554, quoting Shildrick.

7. Bill Hughes, "Being Disabled: Towards a Critical Social Ontology for Disability Studies," *Disability Studies Quarterly* 22, no. 7 (December 2007): 673–84.

8. Bill Hughes, "Wounded/Monstrous/Abject: A Critique of the Disabled Body in the Sociological Imaginary," *Disability & Society* 24, no. 4 (2009): 399–410, 402.

9. Ibid.

10. Martin Ostapczuk and Jochen Musch, "Estimating the Prevalence of Negative Attitudes towards People with Disability: A Comparison of Direct Questioning, Projective Questioning and Randomised Response," *Disability and Rehabilitation* 33, no. 5 (2011): 399–411.

11. According to the American Association on Intellectual and Developmental Disabilities, intellectual disability (formerly known as mental retardation) "originates before the age of 18," and developmental disabilities (such as

fetal alcohol syndrome, Down syndrome, or autism) "are acknowledged during early childhood" (www.aaidd.org).

12. Ladelle McWhorter, *Racism and Sexual Oppression in Anglo-America: A Genealogy* (Bloomington: Indiana University Press, 2009).

13. Adriana S. Benzaquén, *Encounters with Wild Children: Temptation and Disappointment in the Study of Human Nature* (Montreal: McGill–Queen's University Press, 2006); Julia V. Douthwaite, *The Wild Girl, Natural Man, and the Monster: Dangerous Experiments in the Age of Enlightenment* (Chicago: University of Chicago Press, 2002).

14. Jean-Marc-Gaspard Itard, *The Wild Boy of Aveyron* (Englewood Cliffs, N.J.: Prentice-Hall, [1802] 1962), 142.

15. Ibid., 6.

16. Ibid., 11.

17. Ibid., 21–22.

18. Ibid., 20.

19. Ibid., 45.

20. Ibid., 39.

21. Ibid., 40.

22. Ibid., 50.

23. Ibid., 124.

24. Ibid., 57.

25. Ibid., 106, 69.

26. Ibid., 37

27. Ibid., 48.

28. Ibid., 45.

29. Ibid., 46.

30. Ibid., 50.

31. Ibid., 53.

32. Ibid., 128.

33. Ibid., 143.

34. Ibid., 50–51.

35. J. F. Blumenbach, "Contributions to Natural History," in *Anthropological Treatises of Blumenbach and Hunter* (London: Anthropological Society, 1865).

36. Julia V. Douthwaite, "*Homo Ferus*: Between Monster and Model," *Eighteenth-Century Life* 21, no. 2 (1997): 176–202, 193.

37. Quoted in Edouard Séguin, *Idiocy: And Its Treatment by the Physiological Method* (online edition, New York: Teachers College, Columbia University), 22, https://archive.org/details/idiocyitstreatmeoosegu.

38. Michael Newton, *Savage Girls and Wild Boys: A History of Feral Children* (New York: Picador, 2002), 127.

39. David T. Mitchell and Sharon L. Snyder, "Compulsory Feralization: Institutionalizing Disability Studies," *PMLA* 120, no. 2 (2005): 627–34.

40. William B. Fish, "A Thesis on Idiocy," in *Mental Retardation in America: A Historical Reader,* ed. Steven Noll and James W. Trent Jr. (New York: New York University Press, 2004), 29. On the rise of disability as a national problem in the United States in the nineteenth century, see Nielsen, *A Disability History of the United States.*

41. David Wright, *Mental Disability in Victorian England: The Earlswood Asylum, 1847–1901* (Oxford: Oxford University Press, 2001).

42. Mark Jackson, *The Borderland of Imbecility: Medicine, Society and the Fabrication of the Feeble Mind in Late Victorian and Edwardian England* (Manchester: Manchester University Press, 2000), 22.

43. Ibid., 23.

44. Ibid.

45. Ibid., 23.

46. Ibid., 37.

47. Ibid., 24.

48. Lilian Serife Zihni, "The History of the Relationship between the Concept and Treatment of People with Down's Syndrome in Britain and America from 1866–1967" (PhD diss., University College London, 1989), 35.

49. John Langdon Down, *On Some of the Mental Affections of Childhood and Youth: The Lettsomian Lectures Delivered before the Medical Society of London in 1887* (London: J & A Churchill, 1887), https://archive.org.

50. O. C. Ward, "John Langdon Down: The Man and the Message," *Down Syndrome Research and Practice* 6, no. 1 (1999): 19–24.

51. Down, *On Some of the Mental Affections.*

52. David Wright, "Mongols in Our Midst: John Langdon Down and the Ethnic Classification of Idiocy, 1858–1924," in *Mental Retardation in America: A Historical Reader,* ed. Steven Noll and James W. Trent Jr. (New York: New York University Press, 2004), 92–119.

53. John Langdon Down, "Observations on an Ethnic Classification of Idiots," *London Hospital Reports* 3 (1866): 259–62, 260.

54. Ibid.

55. Cynthia Hamilton, "'Am I Not a Man and a Brother?' Phrenology and Anti-slavery," *Slavery & Abolition* 29, no. 2 (2008): 173–87; Nancy Leys Stepan, "Race and Gender: The Role of Analogy in Science," *Isis* 77, no. 2 (June 1986): 261–77.

56. Down, *On Some of the Mental Affections,* 9.

57. Ibid.

58. Quoted in Zihni, "The History of the Relationship," 38.

59. Down, *On Some of the Mental Affections*, 135.

60. Ibid., 130–31.

61. Ibid., 14–15, 41.

62. Ibid., 297.

63. Ibid., 291.

64. Wright, "Mongols in Our Midst"; Daniel J. Kevles, "'Mongolian Imbecility': Race and Its Rejection in the Understanding of Mental Disease," in *Mental Retardation in America: A Historical Reader*, ed. Steven Noll and James W. Trent Jr. (New York: New York University Press, 2004), 120–27.

65. Chris Borthwick, "Idiot into Ape," in *Expanding the Scope of Social Science Research on Disability*, ed. Barbara Mandell Altman and Sharon N. Barnartt (Bingley, UK: Emerald JAI, 2000), 31–54, 35.

66. W. G. Crookshank, *The Mongol in Our Midst: A Study of Man and His Three Faces* (New York: E. P. Dutton & Company, 1924); W. L. Brown, "The Mongol in Our Midst," *Eugenics Review* 23, no. 3 (1931): 251–53.

67. Trent, *Inventing the Feeble Mind*.

68. Nielsen, *A Disability History of the United States*.

69. Henry H. Goddard, *The Kallikak Family: A Study in the Heredity of Feeble-Mindedness* (New York: Macmillan, 1912).

70. Ibid., 72.

71. Ibid., 163.

72. Ibid., 164.

73. Ibid., 29–30.

74. Ibid., 70–71.

75. Henry H. Goddard, "Who Is a Moron?," *Scientific Monthly* 24 no. 1 (1927): 41–46.

76. Goddard, *The Kallikak Family*, 11.

77. Ibid., 12.

78. McWhorter, *Racism and Sexual Oppression*, 138; Trent, *Inventing the Feeble Mind*, 179.

79. McWhorter, *Racism and Sexual Oppression*, 138; Trent, *Inventing the Feeble Mind*, 168.

80. Goddard, *The Kallikak Family*, 78.

81. A recent article exposed how girls and women in a Baltimore institution for the feebleminded were "given" to wealthy families to use as free and permanent labor. Jesse Bering, "A Forgotten Scandal in Baltimore's High Society," *Slate*, March 17, 2014, www.slate.com/articles/health_and_science/medical_examiner/2014/03/baltimore_s_rosewood_scandal_wealthy_families_sprang_asylum_inmates_to_be.html.

82. Goddard, *The Kallikak Family*, 105–6.

83. Licia Carlson, "Cognitive Ableism and Disability Studies: Feminist Reflections on the History of Mental Retardation," *Hypatia* 16, no. 4 (2001): 124–46, 129.

84. Goddard, "Who Is a Moron?," 44–45.

85. Goddard, *The Kallikak Family*, 71.

86. Quoted in Alexander Sanger, "Eugenics, Race, and Margaret Sanger Revisited: Reproductive Freedom for All?," *Hypatia* 22, no. 2 (Spring 2007): 210–17, 212.

87. Trent, *Inventing the Feeble Mind*, 193–95.

88. Harold Pollack, "Learning to Walk Slow: America's Partial Policy Success in the Arena of Intellectual Disability," *Journal of Policy History* 19, no. 1 (January 2007): 95–112, 97.

89. Michael A. Rembis, *Defining Deviance: Sex, Science, and Delinquent Girls, 1890–1960* (Urbana: University of Illinois Press, 2011).

90. Goddard, *The Kallikak Family*, 56.

91. Carlson, "Cognitive Ableism and Disability Studies," 127.

92. Louise Michele Newman, "Women's Rights, Race and Imperialism, 1870–1920," in *Race, Nation and Empire in American History*, ed. James Campbell, Matthew Pratt Guterl, and Robert G. Lee (Chapel Hill: University of North Carolina Press, 2006), 157–80.

93. Nicola Beisel and Tamara Kay, "Abortion, Race, and Gender in Nineteenth-Century America," *American Sociological Review* 69 (August 2004): 498–518. See Rembis, *Defining Deviance*, on the important role that women played in the institutionalization of poor women.

94. Paul A. Lombardo, *Three Generations, No Imbeciles: Eugenics, the Supreme Court, and Buck v. Bell* (Baltimore: Johns Hopkins University Press, 2008); *Buck v. Bell*, 274 U.S. 200 (1927).

95. Douglas Baynton, "Disability and the Justification of Inequality in American History," in *The New Disability History: American Perspectives*, ed. Paul K. Longmore and Lauri Umansky (New York: New York University Press, 2000), 33–57.

96. Kansas City Historical Society, "Cool Things: *American Woman and Her Political Peers* Painting," November 1999 (modified October 2012), www.kshs.org/kansapedia/cool-things-american-woman-and-her-political-peers-painting/10294.

97. James I. Charlton, *Nothing about Us without Us: Disability Oppression and Empowerment* (Berkeley: University of California Press, 1998).

98. Ibid., 17.

99. Quoted in Doris Zames Fleischer and Frieda Zames, *The Disability Rights Movement: From Charity to Confrontation* (Philadelphia: Temple University Press, 2001), 109.

100. R. R. Anspach, "From Stigma to Identity Politics: Political Activism among the Physically Disabled and Former Mental Patients," *Social Science & Medicine* 13 (1979): 765–73.

101. Researchers point out that establishing these kinds of self-concepts may prove especially difficult for people with cognitive disabilities. Michael Finlay and Evanthia Lyons, "Social Identity and People with Learning Difficulties: Implications for Self-Advocacy Groups," *Disability & Society* 13, no. 1 (1998): 37–51.

102. Cary Wolfe, "Learning from Temple Grandin, or, Animal Studies, Disability Studies, and Who Comes after the Subject," *New Formations* 64, no. 1 (2008): 110–23, 118. See also Christine Kelly, "Wrestling with Group Identity: Disability Activism and Direct Funding," *Disability Studies Quarterly* 30, no. 3/4 (2010), www.dsq-sds.org/article/view/1279.

103. Wolfe, "Learning from Temple Grandin," 122.

104. Carole Pateman and Charles Mills, eds., *Contract and Domination* (Cambridge: Polity Press, 2007).

105. Charles Mills, "Intersecting Contracts," in *Contract and Domination*, ed. Carole Pateman and Charles Mills (Cambridge: Polity Press, 2007), 165–99.

106. Pateman, "Race, Sex, and Indifference."

107. Ibid., 137.

108. Ibid., 151–52.

109. Snyder and Mitchell, *Cultural Locations of Disability*, 17; David Mitchell and Sharon Snyder, "Introduction: Disability and the Double Bind of Representation," in *The Body and Physical Difference: Discourses of Disability*, ed. David Mitchell and Sharon Snyder (Ann Arbor: University of Michigan Press, 1997), 1–31, 6. See also Cora Kaplan, "Afterword: Liberalism, Feminism, and Defect," in *"Defects": Engendering the Modern Body*, ed. Helen Deutsch and Felicity Nussbaum (Ann Arbor: University of Michigan Press, 2000), 303–18.

110. Snyder and Mitchell, *Cultural Locations of Disability*, 17.

111. David Mitchell and Sharon Snyder, "The Eugenic Atlantic: Race, Disability, and the Making of an International Eugenic Science, 1800–1945," *Disability & Society* 18, no. 7 (2003): 843–64.

112. Iris Marion Young, *Justice and the Politics of Difference* (Princeton: Princeton University Press, 1990).

113. Pateman, *The Sexual Contract*, 2.

114. Kari Arrayan, *Disability Justice Initiative Technical Report #1: Review of the Literature* (Minot: North Dakota Center for Persons with Disabilities, 2003), 1–17.

115. Carole Pateman, "The Settler Contract," in *Contract and Domination*, ed. Carole Pateman and Charles Mills (Cambridge: Polity Press, 2007), 39.

116. Ibid.

117. Stefan Dolgert, "Species of Disability: Response to Arneil," *Political Theory* 38, no. 6 (December 2010): 859.

3. The Disavowal of Disability in Contemporary Contract Theory

1. Dale Larson, "Unconsciously Regarded as Disabled: Implicit Bias and the Regarded-As Prong of the Americans with Disabilities Act," *UCLA Law Review* 56 (2008): 451–88, 477.

2. Brien A. Nosek, Frederick L. Smyth, Jeffrey J. Hansen, Thierry Devos, Nicole M. Lindner, Kate A. Ranganath, Colin Tucker Smith, Kristina R. Olson, Dolly Chuch, Anthony G. Greenwalk, and Mahzarin R. Banaji, "Pervasiveness and Correlates of Implicit Attitudes and Stereotypes," *European Review of Social Psychology* 18, no. 1 (2007): 1–53.

3. Christian S. Crandall, Amy Eshelman, and Laurie O'Brien, "Social Norms and the Expression and Suppression of Prejudice: The Struggle for Internalization," *Journal of Personality and Social Psychology* 82, no. 3 (2002): 359–78.

4. Gary N. Siperstein, Jennifer Norins, Stephen Corbin, and Timothy Shriver, "Multinational Study of Attitudes toward Individuals with Intellectual Disabilities," *Journal of Policy and Practice in Intellectual Disabilities* 3, no. 2 (2006): 143.

5. On equality, see Kittay, *Love's Labor.* On trust, see Anita Silvers and Leslie Pickering Francis, "Justice through Trust: Disability and the 'Outlier Problem' in Social Contract Theory," *Ethics* 116, no. 1 (2005): 40. On citizenship, see Sophia Isako Wong, "Duties of Justice to Citizens with Cognitive Disabilities," *Metaphilosophy* 40, no. 3–4 (2009): 382–401. On cooperation, see Christie Hartley, "Justice for the Disabled: A Contractualist Approach," *Journal of Social Philosophy* 40, no. 1 (2009): 17–36.

6. John Rawls, "Distributive Justice," in *Collected Papers,* ed. Samuel Freeman (Cambridge, Mass.: Harvard University Press, [1967] 1999), 130–53, 131.

7. Rawls, *A Theory of Justice,* 18; Rawls, *Political Liberalism,* 20.

8. Rawls, *Political Liberalism,* 21.

9. McRuer, *Crip Theory,* 10.

10. Davis, *Enforcing Normalcy,* 8.

11. Mitchell and Snyder, "The Eugenic Atlantic," 843–64, 861.

12. John Rawls, *Justice as Fairness: A Restatement* (Cambridge, Mass.: Belknap Press of Harvard University Press, 2001), 18, 21.

13. Ibid., 272.

14. John Rawls, "Outline of a Decision Procedure for Ethics," in *Collected Papers,* ed. Samuel Freeman (Cambridge, Mass.: Harvard University Press, [1951] 1999), 1–19, 2.

15. Rawls, "Distributive Justice," 259; see also *A Theory of Justice*, 84.

16. Rawls, *A Theory of Justice*, 84.

17. John Rawls, "Constitutional Liberty and the Concept of Justice," in *Collected Papers*, ed. Samuel Freeman (Cambridge, Mass.: Harvard University Press, [1963] 1999), 73–95, 81.

18. Ibid., 82.

19. Ibid.

20. John Rawls, "Distributive Justice: Some Addenda," in *Collected Papers*, ed. Samuel Freeman (Cambridge, Mass.: Harvard University Press, [1968] 1999), 154–75, 163.

21. Rawls, *A Theory of Justice*, 84.

22. Ibid., 85.

23. Amartya Sen, "Poor, Relatively Speaking," Oxford Economic Papers 35, no. 2 (July 1983): 153–69. Also, Amartya Sen, "Justice: Means versus Freedoms," *Philosophy & Public Affairs* 19, no. 2 (Spring 1990): 111–21.

24. Rawls, *A Theory of Justice*, 86.

25. Ibid., 87.

26. On criticisms of biological determinism, see David Moore, "A Very Little Bit of Knowledge: Re-evaluating the Meaning of the Heritability of IQ," *Human Development* 49, no. 6 (2007): 347–53; Richard Lerner, "Another Nine-Inch Nail for Behavioral Genetics!," *Human Development* 49, no. 6 (2007): 336–42.

27. D. Daiches Raphael, "Justice and Liberty," *Proceedings of the Aristotelian Society* 51 (1950): 167–96; Herbert Spiegelberg, "A Defense of Human Equality," *Philosophical Review* 53, no. 2 (1944): 101–24.

28. Rawls, *A Theory of Justice*, 86.

29. Raphael, "Justice and Liberty," 187–88.

30. Ibid., 189.

31. Ibid.

32. Rawls, "Distributive Justice," 166; *A Theory of Justice*, 86.

33. Spiegelberg, "A Defense of Human Equality," 120.

34. Ibid., 19.

35. Rawls, *A Theory of Justice*, 86.

36. Francis Galton, *English Men of Science: Their Nature and Nurture* (New York: D. Appleton and Company, 1875); Francis Galton, "Eugenics: Its Definition, Scope, and Aims," *American Journal of Sociology* 10, no. 1 (1904): 1–25.

37. Rawls, *A Theory of Justice*, 92.

38. Ibid.

39. Ibid., 92–93.

40. Nussbaum, *Frontiers of Justice*, 100.

41. Hartley, "Disability and Justice," 120–32, 120; Carlson and Kittay, "Introduction," 307–30, 310.

42. David Mitchell and Sharon Snyder, *Narrative Prosthesis: Disability and the Dependencies of Discourse* (Ann Arbor: University of Michigan Press, 2000).

43. Arneil, "Disability, Self Image, and Modern Political Thought," 1–25.

44. Sophia Isako Wong, "Duties of Justice to Citizens with Cognitive Disabilities," *Metaphilosophy* 40, no. 3–4 (2009): 382–401; Christie Hartley, "Disability and Justice," *Philosophy Compass* 6, no. 2 (2011): 120–32; Christie Hartley, "Justice for the Disabled: A Contractualist Approach," *Journal of Social Philosophy* 40, no. 1 (2009): 17–36; Silvers and Francis, "Justice through Trust," 40.

45. Hartley, "Justice for the Disabled," 28; emphasis in the original.

46. Ibid., 28–29.

47. Research shows that people with intellectual and developmental disabilities have very limited social networks. Rachel Forrester-Jones, John Carpenter, Pauline Coolen-Schrijner, Paul Cambridge, Alison Tate, Jennifer Beecham, Angela Hallam, Martin Knapp, and David Wooff, "The Social Networks of People with Intellectual Disability Living in the Community 12 Years after Resettlement from Long-Stay Hospitals," *Journal of Applied Research in Intellectual Disabilities* 19 (2006): 285–95; Tessa Lippold and Jan Burns, "Social Support and Intellectual Disabilities: A Comparison between Social Networks of Adults with Intellectual Disability and Those with Physical Disability," *Journal of Intellectual Disability Research* 53, no. 5 (2009): 463–73.

48. Hartley, "Justice for the Disabled," 30–31.

49. Nussbaum, *Frontiers of Justice*, 181.

50. Silvers and Francis, "Justice through Trust," 43.

51. Ibid., 74.

52. Charles W. Mills, "Rawls on Race / Race in Rawls," *Southern Journal of Philosophy* 47 (2009): 161–84, 162.

53. Mills, "'Ideal Theory' as Ideology," 165–84, 169.

54. Mills, *The Racial Contract*, 18.

55. Ibid., 95.

56. Ibid., 97.

57. Ibid., 92.

58. Ibid.

59. Ibid., 119.

60. Carlson, "Philosophers of Intellectual Disability," 552–66.

61. Young, "Taking the Basic Structure Seriously," 91–97, 95.

62. Ibid.

63. Mills, "Rawls on Race / Race in Rawls," 161–84.

64. Mills, "'Ideal Theory' as Ideology."

65. Hilary White, "Half of Americans Would Choose Death over Disability: Survey," July 15, 2008, www.lifesitenews.com/news/half-of-americans-would-choose-death-over-disability-survey.

66. Feminist theorists who refer to the wheelchair user as a model for emancipatory politics include Young, "Taking the Basic Structure Seriously"; Ackerly, *Universal Human Rights in a World of Difference*; Nancy J. Hirschmann, "Rawls, Freedom, and Disability: A Feminist Rereading," in *Feminist Interpretations of John Rawls*, ed. Ruth Abbey (University Park: Pennsylvania State University Press, 2013), 96–114.

67. Mitchell L. Yell, David Rogers, and Elisabeth Lodge Rodgers, "The Legal History of Special Education: What a Long, Strange Trip It's Been!," *Remedial & Special Education* 19, no. 4 (July/August 1998), 219–28, 220.

68. Ibid.

69. Janet Robertson, Eric Emerson, Lisa Pinkney, Emma Caesar, David Felce, Andrea Meek, Deborah Carr, Kathy Lowe, Martin Knapp, and Angela Hallam, "Community-Based Residential Supports for People with Intellectual Disabilities and Challenging Behavior: The Views of Neighbors," *Journal of Applied Research in Intellectual Disabilities* 18 (2005): 85–92.

70. Kittay, *Love's Labor*; Wong, "At Home with Down Syndrome and Gender," 89–117; Wong, "Duties of Justice to Citizens with Cognitive Disabilities."

71. Eva Feder Kittay, "The Personal Is Philosophical Is Political: A Philosopher and Mother of a Cognitively Disabled Person Sends Notes from the Battlefield," *Metaphilosophy* 40, no. 3–4 (2009): 606–27.

72. Kittay, "The Personal Is Philosophical Is Political," 617.

73. Ibid., 563.

4. Rethinking Political Agency

1. I have chosen to use the real name of Max Burrows, since he is a leader in the self-advocacy movement and has therefore taken a public role in relation to these issues.

2. People First of West Virginia, www.peoplefirstwv.org.

3. People First of Washington, www.peoplefirstsv.com/people_first_history.htm.

4. People First of California, www.peoplefirstca.org/about_philosphy.html.

5. Griet Roets and Dan Goodley, "Disability, Citizenship and Uncivilized Society: The Smooth and Nomadic Qualities of Self-Advocacy," *Disability Studies Quarterly* 28, no. 4 (2008), http://dsq-sds.org/article/view/131/131.

6. Allison C. Carey, *On the Margins of Citizenship: Intellectual Disability and Civil Rights in Twentieth-Century America* (Philadelphia: Temple University Press, 2009), 223.

7. Originally the National Association for Retarded Children, it later changed its name to the Association for Retarded Citizens of the United States, and is now known as The Arc.

8. Michael Wehmeyer, Hank Bersani Jr., and Ray Gagne, "Riding the Third Wave: Self-Determination and Self-Advocacy in the 21st Century," *Focus on Autism and Other Developmental Disabilities* 15, no. 2 (Summer 2000): 106–15.

9. Doris Zames Fleischer and Frieda Zames, *The Disability Rights Movement: From Charity to Confrontation* (Philadelphia: Temple University Press, 2001), 113.

10. Frank Bylov, "Patterns of Culture and Power after the Great Release: The History of Movements of Sub Culture and Empowerment among Danish People with Learning Difficulties," *British Journal of Learning Disabilities* 34 (2006): 139–45.

11. Derrick Armstrong, "The Politics of Self-Advocacy and People with Learning Difficulties," *Policy & Politics* 30, no. 3 (2002): 333–45.

12. Mary F. Hayden and Tia Nelis, "Self-Advocacy," in *Embarking on a New Century: Mental Retardation at the End of the 20th Century,* ed. Robert L. Schalock, Pamela C. Baker, and M. Doreen Croser (Washington D.C.: American Association on Mental Retardation, 2002), 221–33.

13. People First of West Virginia, http://peoplefirstwv.org/people-first /about/history.html.

14. Jan Walmsley and the Central England People First History Project Team, "Telling the History of Self-Advocacy: A Challenge for Inclusive Research," *Journal of Applied Research in Intellectual Disabilities* 27 (2014): 34–43.

15. Lisa Vanhala, *Making Rights a Reality? Disability Rights Activists and Legal Mobilization* (Oxford: Oxford University Press, 2011).

16. Ibid.

17. People First of Oregon, "What Is People First?," www.peoplefirst.org.

18. Lisa Vanhala, *Making Rights a Reality?*

19. Joe Caldwell, "Leadership Development of Individuals with Developmental Disabilities in the Self-Advocacy Movement," *Journal of Intellectual Disability Research* 54, no. 11 (2010): 1004–1014.

20. Carey, *On the Margins of Citizenship,* 167.

21. Joey Sprague and Jeanne Hayes, "Self-Determination and Empowerment: A Feminist Standpoint Analysis of Talk about Disability," *American Journal of Community Psychology* 28, no. 5 (2000): 671; Carey, *On the Margins of Citizenship.*

22. Kristin Bumiller, "Quirky Citizens: Autism, Gender, and Reimagining Disability," *Signs* 33, no. 4 (Summer 2008): 967–91.

23. Carey, *On the Margins of Citizenship,* 176.

24. Ibid.

25. Colin Goble, "Dependence, Independence and Normality," in *Disabling Barriers—Enabling Environments,* ed. John Swain, Sally French, Colin Barnes, and Carol Thomas (London: Sage, 2014), 35.

26. Ibid., 138.

27. Wehmeyer et al., "Riding the Third Wave," 112.

28. Vanhala, *Making Rights a Reality?*

29. Ibid. See also Eygló Ebba Hreinsdóttir, Guðún Stefánsdóttir, Anne Lewthwaite, Sue Ledger, and Lindy Shufflebotham, "Is My Story So Different from Yours? Comparing Life Stories, Experiences of Institutionalization and Self-Advocacy in England and Iceland," *British Journal of Learning Disabilities* 34, no. 3 (September 2006): 157–66.

30. Louise Townson, Sue Macauley, Elizatbeth Harkness, Andy Docherty, John Dias, Malcolm Eadley, and Rohhs Chapman, "Research Project on Advocacy and Autism," *Disability & Society* 22, no. 5 (2007): 523–36; Melanie Chapman, Susan Bannister, Julie Davies, Simon Fleming, Claire Graham, Andrea Mcmaster, Angela Seddon, Anita Wheldom, and Bridget Whittell, "Speaking Up about Advocacy: Findings from a Partnership Research Project," *British Journal of Learning Disabilities* 40 (2011): 71–80; Rannbeig Traustadóttir, "Learning about Self-Advocacy from Life History: A Case Study from the United States," *British Journal of Learning Disabilities* 34 (2006): 175–80.

31. Stacy L. Nonnemacher and Linda M. Bambara, "'I'm Supposed to Be In Charge': Self-Advocates' Perspectives on Their Self-Determination Support Needs," *Intellectual and Developmental Disabilities* 49, no. 5 (2011): 327–40, 331.

32. Ibid., 320.

33. Andrew Gilmartin and Eamonn Slevin, "Being a Member of a Self-Advocacy Group: Experiences of Intellectually Disabled People," *British Journal of Learning Disabilities* 38, no. 3 (September 2010): 152–59, 156.

34. Eiji Tsuda and John Smith, "Defining and Organizing Self-Advocate Centered Groups: Implications of Survey Research on Self-Advocacy Groups in Japan," *Disability & Society* 19, no. 6 (2004): 627–46.

35. Edurne Garcia-Iriarte, John C. Kramer, Jessica M. Kramer, and Jay Hammel, "'Who Did What?' A Participatory Action Research Project to Increase Group Capacity for Advocacy," *Journal of Applied Research in Intellectual Disabilities* 22, no. 1 (2009): 10–22; Dan Goodley, "'Learning Difficulties,' the Social Model of Disability and Impairment: Challenging Epistemologies," *Disability & Society* 16, no. 2 (2001): 207–31.

36. Ian Buchanan and Jan Walmsley, "Self-Advocacy in Historical Perspective," *British Journal of Learning Disabilities* 34, no. 3 (2006): 133–38; Simone Aspis, "Self-Advocacy for People with Learning Difficulties: Does It Have a Future?," *Disability & Society* 12, no. 4 (1997): 647–54.

37. Goodley, "'Learning Difficulties,' the Social Model of Disability and Impairment"; Sprague and Hayes, "Self-Determination and Empowerment"; Garcia-Iriarte et al., "'Who Did What?'"

38. Chapman et al., "Speaking Up about Advocacy."

39. Gilmartin and Slevin, "Being a Member of a Self-Advocacy Group."

40. Eiji Tsuda, "Japanese Culture and the Philosophy of Self-Advocacy: The Importance of Interdependence in Community Living," *British Journal of Learning Disabilities* 34 (2006): 151–56.

41. Margrit Shildrick, "Becoming Vulnerable: Contagious Encounters and the Ethics of Risk," *Journal of Medical Humanities* 21, no. 4 (2000): 215–27, 219; Michelle Jarman, "Resisting 'Good Imperialism': Reading Disability as Radical Vulnerability," *Atenea* 25, no. 1 (2005): 107–16.

42. Carey, *On the Margins of Citizenship*.

43. Seyla Benhabib, *Situating the Self: Gender, Community and Postmodernism in Contemporary Ethics* (New York: Routledge, 1992), 11; Margaret Canovan, "The Contradictions of Hannah Arendt's Political Thought," *Political Theory* 6, no. 1 (February 1978): 5–26.

44. Hannah Arendt, *Responsibility and Judgment* (New York: Schocken Books, 2003), 5.

45. Hannah Arendt, *The Human Condition* (Chicago: University of Chicago Press, [1958] 1998), 180.

46. Ibid., 206.

47. Ibid., 181.

48. Ibid., 40.

49. Ibid., 221, 237.

50. Ibid., 234.

51. Ibid., 188, 233.

52. Ibid., 182.

53. Ibid., 213.

54. Margaret Canovan, *Hannah Arendt: A Reinterpretation of Her Political Thought* (Cambridge: Cambridge University Press, 1992), 147.

55. Arendt, *The Human Condition*, 190.

56. Ibid., 200.

57. Ibid., 198.

58. Cristina Beltrán, "Going Public: Hannah Arendt, Immigrant Action, and the Space of Appearance," *Political Theory* 37, no. 5 (October 2009): 595–622, 602. I inserted "disability" in place of "rightlessness."

59. Arendt, *The Human Condition*, 58.

60. Ibid., 57.

61. Ibid., 178–79.

62. Ibid., 178.

63. Stacy Clifford, "Making Disability Public in Deliberative Democracy," *Contemporary Political Theory* 11, no. 2 (2012): 211–28.

64. Nonnemacher and Bambara, "'I'm Supposed to Be in Charge"; Gurit Lotan and Carolyn Ells, "Adults with Intellectual and Developmental Disabili-

ties and Participation in Decision Making: Ethical Considerations for Professional–Client Practice," *Intellectual and Developmental Disabilities* 48, no. 2 (2010): 112–25; Michael L. Wehmeyer and Susan B. Palmer, "Adult Outcomes for Students with Cognitive Disabilities: Three-Years after High School: The Impact of Self-Determination," *Education and Training in Developmental Disabilities* 38, no. 2 (2003): 131–44; Roger J. Stancliffe, "Living with Support in the Community: Predictors of Choice and Self-Determination," *Mental Retardation and Developmental Disabilities Research Reviews* 7, no. 2 (2001): 91–98.

65. Barney G. Glaser and Anselm L. Strauss, "Theoretical Sampling," in *Discovery of Grounded Theory: Strategies for Qualitative Research* (New York: Aldine de Gruyter, 1967); Roy Suddaby, "From the Editors: What Grounded Theory Is Not," *Academy of Management Journal* 49, no. 4 (2006): 633–42; Arthur P. Bochner, "Narrative's Virtues," *Qualitative Inquiry* 7, no. 2 (2001): 131–57.

66. Hannah Arendt, *Between Past and Future* (London: Faber & Faber, 1961), 14.

67. Kathy Charmaz, *Constructing Grounded Theory: A Practical Guide through Qualitative Analysis* (Thousand Oaks, Calif.: Sage Publications, 2006).

68. Jenny Slater, "Self-Advocacy and Socially Just Pedagogy," *Disability Studies Quarterly* 32, no. 1 (2012), http://dsq-sds.org/article/view/3033; Roets and Goodley, "Disability, Citizenship and Uncivilized Society"; Jo Aldridge, "Picture This: The Use of Participatory Photographic Research Methods with People with Learning Disabilities," *Disability & Society* 22, no. 1 (2007): 1–17; Stephanie J. Brewster, "Putting Words into Their Mouths? Interviewing People with Learning Disabilities and Little/No Speech," *British Journal of Learning Disabilities* 32, no. 4 (2004): 166–69.

69. Griet Roets, Dan Goodley, and Geert Van Hove, "Narrative in a Nutshell: Sharing Hopes, Fears, and Dreams with Self-Advocates," *Intellectual and Developmental Disabilities* 45, no. 5 (2007): 323–34; Griet Roets and Geert Van Hove, "The Story of Belle, Minnie, Louise and the Sovjets: Throwing Light on the Dark Side of an Institution," *Disability & Society* 18, no. 5 (2003): 599–624.

70. Arendt, *The Human Condition*, 191–92.

71. Christine Bigby, Marie Knox, Julie Beadle-Brown, Tim Clement, and Jim Mansell, "Uncovering Dimensions of Culture in Underperforming Group Homes for People with Severe Intellectual Disability," *Intellectual and Developmental Disabilities* 50, no. 6 (2012): 452–67.

72. Roy McConkey and Suzanne Collins, "The Role of Support Staff in Promoting the Social Inclusion of Persons with an Intellectual Disability," *Journal of Intellectual Disability Research* 54, no. 8 (2010): 691–700.

73. Ibid.

74. Other scholars of disability note the positive power of teasing and laughter. In a study of families with children with disabilities, Rieger differentiates

harsh and hurtful teasing from the kinds of teasing she documented in families. For one father, "'Those who love each other tease each other.'" Alicja Rieger, "Explorations of the Functions of Humor and Other Types of Fun among Families of Children with Disabilities," *Research & Practice for Persons with Severe Disabilities* 29, no. 3 (2004): 194–209, 203.

75. Karl Numkoosing and Mark Hayden-Laurelut, "Intellectual Disability Trouble: Foucault and Goffman on 'Challenging Behavior,'" in *Disability and Social Theory: New Developments and Directions*, ed. Dan Goodley, Bill Hughes, and Lennard Davis (New York: Palgrave Macmillan, 2012), 195–211, 200.

76. Arendt, *The Human Condition*, 55, quoting Barrows.

77. Giles Perring, "The Facilitation of Learning-Disabled Arts: A Cultural Perspective," in *Bodies in Commotion: Disability and Performance*, ed. Carrie Sandahl and Philip Auslinger (Ann Arbor: University of Michigan Press, 2005), 175–89, 184.

78. Lennard J. Davis, "Why Is Disability Missing from the Discourse on Diversity?," *Chronicle of Higher Education*, September 25, 2011, http://chronicle .com/article/Why-Is-Disability-Missing-From/129088.

79. Anne Mollow, "Identity Politics and Disability Studies: A Critique of Recent Theory," *Michigan Quarterly Review* 43, no. 2 (2004), http://hdl.handle .net/2027/spo.act2080.0043.218.

80. Arendt, *The Human Condition*, 177–78.

5. Self-Advocates and Allies Becoming Empowered

1. Ellis and Bochner, "Telling and Performing Personal Stories."

2. Kittay, "The Personal Is Philosophical Is Political," 606–27.

3. Hilary Johnson, Jacinta Douglas, Christine Bigby, and Teresa Iacono, "Social Interaction with Adults with Severe Intellectual Disability: Having Fun and Hanging Out," *Journal of Applied Research in Intellectual Disabilities* 25 (2009): 329–41.

4. *Vital Signs: Crip Culture Talks Back*, directed by Sharon L. Snyder and David T. Mitchell (Boston: Fanlight Productions, 1995), DVD.

5. On changing public space through the appearance of disability, see Rosemarie Garland-Thomson, *Staring: How We Look* (Oxford: Oxford University Press, 2009).

6. Carey, *On the Margins of Citizenship*, 184.

7. Ibid.

8. Self Advocates Becoming Empowered, www.sabeusa.org/meet-sabe.

9. Ibid.

10. Paul Longmore, "The Second Phase: From Disability Rights to Disability Culture," Independent Living Institute, September/October 1995, www .independentliving.org/docs3/longm95.html.

11. Marcus Redley and Darin Weinberg, "Learning Disability and the Limits of Liberal Citizenship: Interactional Impediments to Political Empowerment," *Sociology of Health & Illness* 29, no. 5 (2007): 767–86.

12. Keating, *Decolonizing Democracy*.

13. Margaret Price, "Cripping Revolution: A Crazed Essay" (presentation, Society for Disability Studies, San Jose, Calif., June 18, 2011), http://margaret price.wordpress.com/presentations.

14. Rohhs Chapman, "An Exploration of the Self-Advocacy Support Role through Collaborative Research: 'There Should Never Be a Them and Us,'" *Journal of Applied Research in Intellectual Disabilities* 27 (2014): 44–53.

15. Rohhs Chapman and Liz Tilley, "Exploring the Ethical Underpinning of Self-Advocacy Support for Intellectually Disabled Adults," *Ethics and Social Welfare* 7, no. 3 (2013): 257–71.

16. Carrie Sandahl and Philip Auslinger, eds., *Bodies in Commotion: Disability and Performance* (Ann Arbor: University of Michigan Press, 2005), 14.

17. Eva Feder Kittay, *Love's Labor: Essays on Women, Equality, and Dependency* (New York: Routledge, 1999).

18. Brueggemann, "Delivering Disability, Willing Speech."

19. Chapman and Tilley, "Exploring the Ethical Underpinning of Self-Advocacy."

20. Susan Miller Smedema, Deborah Ebener, and Virginia Grist-Gordon, "The Impact of Humorous Media on Attitudes toward Persons with Disabilities," *Disability and Rehabilitation* 34, no. 17 (2012): 1431–37.

21. Johnson et al., "Social Interaction with Adults with Severe Intellectual Disability."

22. Alan Shain, "Perspectives on Comedy and Performance as Radical Disability Activism," *Journal of Literary & Cultural Disability Studies* 7, no. 3 (2013): 337–46.

23. Gary L. Albrecht, "Disability Humor: What's in a Joke?," *Body & Society* 5, no. 4 (1999): 67–74; Jessica Berson, "Performing Deaf Identity: Toward a Continuum of Deaf Performance," in *Bodies in Commotion: Disability and Performance,* ed. Carrie Sandahl and Philip Auslinger (Ann Arbor: University of Michigan Press, 2005), 42–55; Tom Shakespeare, "Joking a Part," *Body & Society* 5, no. 4 (1999): 47–52.

24. Shakespeare, "Joking a Part," 49.

25. Cynthia Barounis, "'Why So Serious?' Cripping Camp Performance in Christopher Nolan's *The Dark Night,*" *Journal of Literary & Cultural Disability Studies* 7, no. 3 (2013): 305–20, 306.

26. Klaus Dodds and Philip Kirby, "It's Not a Laughing Matter: Critical Geopolitics, Humor and Unlaughter," *Geopolitics* 18, no. 1 (2013): 45–59; Shakespeare, "Joking a Part."

27. Shakespeare, "Joking a Part," 48.

28. Sandahl and Auslander, *Bodies in Commotion*, 3.

29. Tom Coogan, "'Usually I Love the *Onion*, but This Time You've Gone Too Far': Disability Humor and Transgression," *Journal of Literary & Cultural Disability Studies* 7, no. 1 (2013): 1–17.

30. Hannah Macpherson, "'I Don't Know Why They Call It the Lake District They Might as Well Call It the Rock District!' The Workings of Humor and Laughter in Research with Members of Visually Impaired Walking Groups," *Environment and Planning D: Society and Space* 26, no. 6 (2008): 1080–95.

31. Arendt, *The Human Condition*, 236–44.

32. Ibid., 234–35.

33. Ibid., 235.

34. Eimir McGrath, "Dancing with Disability: An Intersubjective Approach," in *Disability and Social Theory: New Developments and Directions*, ed. Dan Goodley, Bill Hughes, and Lennard Davis (New York: Palgrave Macmillan, 2012), 143–58, 143; Ann Cooper Albright, "Strategic Abilities: Negotiating the Disabled Body in Dance," in *Moving History/Dancing Cultures*, ed. Ann Dils and Ann Cooper Albright (Middletown, Conn.: Wesleyan University Press, 2001), 56–66.

35. Petra Kuppers, *Disability and Contemporary Performance: Bodies on Edge* (New York: Routledge, 2003); Owen Smith, "Shifting Apollo's Frame: Challenging the Body Aesthetic in Theater Dance," in *Bodies in Commotion: Disability and Performance*, ed. Carrie Sandhal and Philip Auslinger (Ann Arbor: University of Michigan Press, 2005), 73–85.

36. Giles Perring, "The Facilitation of Learning-Disabled Arts: A Cultural Perspective," in *Bodies in Commotion: Disability and Performance*, ed. Carrie Sandahl and Philip Auslinger (Ann Arbor: University of Michigan Press, 2005), 175–89; Melissa C. Nash, "Beyond Therapy: 'Performance' Work with People Who Have Profound & Multiple Disabilities," in *Bodies in Commotion: Disability and Performance*, ed. Carrie Sandahl and Philip Auslinger (Ann Arbor: University of Michigan Press, 2005), 190–201.

37. Nash, "Beyond Therapy," 192.

38. Ibid., 191.

39. Simi Linton, *My Body Politic: A Memoir* (Ann Arbor: University of Michigan Press, 2007); Rosemarie Garland-Thomson, "Shape Structures Story: Fresh and Feisty Stories about Disability," *Narrative* 15, no. 1 (2007): 113–23; Snyder and Mitchell, *Cultural Locations of Disability*, 200.

40. Sami Schalk, "Coming to Claim Crip: Disidentification with/in Disability Studies," *Disability Studies Quarterly* 33, no. 2 (2013), http://dsq-sds.org/article/view/3705.

41. John Locke, *Of the Conduct of the Understanding* (Bristol, UK: Thoemmes Press, 1993).

42. *Oxford English Dictionary,* www.oed.com.

43. Alicia Rieger, "Explorations of the Functions of Humor and Other Types of Fun among Families of Children with Disabilities," *Research & Practice for Persons with Severe Disabilities* 29, no. 3 (2004): 194–209.

44. Walmsley and the Central England People First History Project Team, "Telling the History of Self-Advocacy," 34–43; Caldwell, "Leadership Development of Individuals with Developmental Disabilities," 1004–14.

45. Ackerly, *Political Theory and Feminist Social Criticism.*

Index

abled/disabled binary: alliances with self-advocates and, 122–25; compulsory capacity and, 65–69; dance and, 129–32; disability studies and destabilization of, 15–16; empowerment in context of, 95; humor and, 125–29; Rawls's theory of justice and, 76–79; self-advocacy movement and, 95–99, 106–15, 120–35; transactions in, 139n.2

ableist norms, anxiety about disability and, 2–4, 47–49

abortion, of Down syndrome fetuses, 9–10, 142n.36

abuse of people with disabilities, exposure of, 12

Ackerly, Brooke, 27, 134

African Americans: history of disability classifications for, 60–63; IQ testing of, 75; Mills's racial contract and, 66; self-advocacy movement and, 106–15, 123–25

Albrecht, Gary L., 125–29

alliance: communication through, 133–35; mobilization against anxiety through, 122–25; self-advocacy and, 23–24, 121–35

American Association on Intellectual and Developmental Disabilities (AAIDD), 8–9, 152n.11

Americans with Disabilities Act, 9, 120; liberal humanist theory and, 65

Anspach, R. R., 65

anxiety about disability: alliance against, 122–25; capacity measurement and, 7–11; care theory and, 11–16; contact with disability and erasure of, 90–92; dance as tool for countering, 129–32; democratic theory and, 21–22; disability studies and, 2–4; Goddard's typology of feeblemindedness and, 58–63; history of disability and, 22, 47–49, 56–58; humor and suspension of, 125–29; identity and, 16–21; measurement of capacity and, 11; medicalization of disability and manufacturing of, 47, 58–63

The Arc, 95, 161n.7

Arendt, Hannah, 23, 95–117; on forgiveness, 128; on freedom, 129; semisovereign subject theory of, 100–103; on spontaneity and public action, 110–15

Association for Retarded Citizens of the United States, 161n.7

Auslander, Philip, 18, 123

authority, Locke on ignorance and, 44–46

STACY CLIFFORD SIMPLICAN is a postdoctoral research fellow at Michigan State University.